TOMAHAWK AND MUSKET

French and Indian Raids in the Ohio Valley 1758

RENÉ CHARTRAND

OSPREY PUBLISHING
Bloomsbury Publishing Plc

Kemp House, Chawley Park, Cumnor Hill, Oxford OX2 9PH, UK
29 Earlsfort Terrace, Dublin 2, Ireland
1385 Broadway, 5th Floor, New York, NY 10018, USA
Email: info@ospreypublishing.com
www.ospreypublishing.com

OSPREY is a trademark of Osprey Publishing Ltd

First published in Great Britain in 2012

A CIP catalog record for this book is available from the British Library.

Print ISBN: 978 1 84908 564 9
ePDF: 978 1 84908 567 0
ePub: 978 1 78096 033 3

Page layout by www.bounford.com
Maps by www.bounford.com
Index by Marie-Pierre Evans
Typeset in Sabon
Originated by United Graphics Pte., Singapore
Printed and bound in India by Replika Press Private Ltd.

22 23 24 25 26   15 14 13 12 11 10 9

Author's acknowledgments
I would like to thank Martin and Penny West of Fort Ligonier in Pennsylvania and the
many helpful colleagues at National Historic Sites of Parks Canada in Ottawa, the Fort Pitt
Museum in Pittsburgh, Library and Archives Canada in Ottawa, The National Archives
of the United Kingdom in Kew, the Archives Nationales in France, the Library of Congress
in Washington, and the Brown University Library in Providence.

Dedication
In memory of William L. Brown III of Maryland. Superlative curator, historian, documentary
film director and friend.

Abbreviations
In brackets for source of document quoted:
Bouquet: *The Papers of Henry Bouquet*
CO: Colonial Office
Cubbison: *The British Defeat of the French in Pennsylvania 1758*
DCHNY: *Documents Relative to the Colonial History of the State of New York*
Forbes: *Writings of General John Forbes*
WO: War Office

The Woodland Trust
Osprey Publishing supports the Woodland Trust, the UK's leading woodland
conservation charity.

www.ospreypublishing.com
To find out more about our authors and books visit our website. Here you will find
extracts, author interviews, details of forthcoming events and the option to sign-up
for our newsletter.

CONTENTS

INTRODUCTION   4

ORIGINS   5

INITIAL STRATEGY   18

THE PLAN   25

GRANT'S RAID ON FORT DUQUESNE   49

AUBRY'S RAID ON FORT LIGONIER   60
Lt. Corbière's patrol on November 12   66

ANALYSIS   70

CONCLUSION   71

FURTHER READING AND BIBLIOGRAPHY   77

INDEX   80

INTRODUCTION

In the histories of the Seven Years' War in North America, the campaign by General Forbes to reach the Ohio Valley in 1758 has always been overshadowed by the more spectacular Ticonderoga campaign and the taking of Louisbourg, both of which occurred during that year; and also by the disastrous 1755 defeat suffered by General Braddock near the Monongahela, so that Forbes' campaign three years later is treated somewhat as an afterthought.

It has to be admitted that the 1758 campaign did not produce a major engagement in a huge battlefield. No great charges; no great generals. Much of the Anglo-American army's activity centered on road- and fort-building. Oddly enough, many accounts and, particularly, American histories of the conflict, seem more fascinated by these construction endeavors than by the fighting that did indeed take place. Perhaps because the one Anglo-American raid on Fort Duquesne, led by Major Grant, turned out to be a monumental fiasco and because the French raid on Fort Ligonier was such a success, to the point where this author suspects some denial on the part of rather patriotic historians. However, the core of the problem is probably the paucity of the accounts regarding both raids. It is remarkably difficult to find good, let alone detailed, first-hand accounts of both actions. There are no precise contemporary maps or illustrations, sometimes no maps at all, of the actions. Historian Douglas R. Cubbison has published a fine account of Forbes' army quoting extensively British and American sources. In this study, we contribute many French accounts to the record, some published for the first time in English.

As readers will see in the following pages, we have had to make many assumptions as to the approximate location of even the general actions during a raid, let alone details on a particular aspect. Some may be open to question, but, on the whole, we hope it gives a good general view of these two very large raids of the last years of what Americans often call the French and Indian War.

ORIGINS

In the middle of the 18th century, North America was claimed and partially occupied by three major European powers: Spain, France, and Great Britain. Spain's domain was largely to the south, encompassing the vast viceroyalty of New Spain that comprised present-day Mexico, Central America, the larger West Indian islands, Florida, and much of the American southwest. This huge territory was not, however, in a great rivalry with the colonies of the other two powers.

New France covered a vast area extending from the Gulf of the St. Lawrence River in Canada to the Rocky Mountains westward and to the Gulf of Mexico southward, forming a sort of huge crescent across the middle of the continent. It was sparsely populated with French settlers, who by the mid-18th century probably numbered no more than 65,000 souls mostly living in Canada along the shores of the St. Lawrence. There were perhaps another five or six thousand more in Louisiana going from the Gulf to Illinois, while about a further four thousand were in the port fortress city of Louisbourg on Cape Breton Island. While agriculture played an important role along the shores of the St. Lawrence, fur was Canada's main export so Canadian fur traders roamed over vast expanses to trade with the Indian nations who were, in fact, the true masters of the primeval forest and the vast rolling prairies.

The smallest group of colonies was the one over which flew Great Britain's flag, which occupied the mainland's seaboard from Nova Scotia to Georgia. These various colonies were originally settled by groups of Englishmen, Dutchmen, and Swedes that had been joined by many Scots and Germans later on. By the middle of the 18th century, the population of the British colonies along the Atlantic seaboard hovered at around a million and a quarter. Many were merchants and seafarers, but most farmed plots of land. The British colonies were extensively settled with farms and plantations, and featured several large cities such as Boston, New York, and Philadelphia. The territories of these colonies were restrained to the east of the Appalachian Mountains. As population grew, the pressure to find new western land increased.

**APRIL 16
1754**

French troops occupy future site of Fort Duquesne

Map of North America in the 1750s. Spain, France, and Great Britain had various claims to substantial parts of America, much of it, such as Rupert's Land or western Canada, unsettled by European powers. (Author's photo)

In terms of military command and of the ability to marshal forces, the far less populous New France had the advantage. It was, since the 1660s, administered by the royal French government and therefore generally organized, with various allowances for place and distance, like a French province. The capital was Quebec City, the port of entry to Canada, and the place of residence of the governor-general, who was both the highest official in New France and the governor of Canada, the most important part of the domain, going from the Gulf of St. Lawrence to the western prairies. On the east coast, Acadia and southern Newfoundland had been lost to Britain by the 1713 Treaty of Utrecht, but France had built the sizable fortress city of Louisbourg on Isle Royale, as Cape Breton Island was then called, and this area was set up as a separate colony with its own governor. Louisiana had been settled from the early 18th century on the shores of the Gulf of Mexico and up the Mississippi River to the Illinois Country south of the Great Lakes, and it had its own governor residing at New Orleans. In matters of command and policy, the governors were the supreme commanders of the forces within their respective colonies; they formulated the diplomatic ties with the Indian nations, and reported to the minister of the navy and colonies in France, who himself reported to the king and was part of his council. It was an autocratic form of government from top to bottom, and while each governor had to have a "superior council" made up of the colony's most eminent civilian and religious leaders, there was no such thing as an elected assembly.

All three of France's North American colonies were each provided with a garrison of regular colonial troops, the Compagnies Franches de la Marine (independent companies of the navy) with a few companies of gunners. Those at Isle Royale were nearly all in Louisbourg. In Canada and Louisiana, a core of these troops were posted in cities such as Quebec, Montreal, Detroit, New Orleans, and Mobile, while the rest were spread out in the many forts built along the French trade routes. By 1758 the official New France military establishment came to 99 regular colonial infantry companies and four artillery companies, making a theoretical total of some five thousand officers and men. But too few recruits and replacements had been sent and the actual strength was probably about a third less. A peculiar feature was that from the late 17th century, and as years went by, the officers of these troops were increasingly born in Canada. By the middle of the 18th century, a large majority of officers were Canadian gentlemen. The enlisted men were recruited in France and after their period of service – officially six years, but this often varied – they were encouraged to settle in Canada or Louisiana. About a quarter to a third of the soldiers were posted in the far-flung wilderness forts. These postings could be for periods of about two years, but some of the soldiers grew fond of life in remote outposts and some appear to have remained there the rest of their lives. When passing at Fort Michilimackinac, gunner J.C.B. (see bibliography) met a Compagnie Franche infantryman who had been there for 25 years. Some of these men became quite at ease in this wilderness environment and assimilated, largely from their Indian allies, the notions of bush warfare.

In New France, every able-bodied male aged from 16 to 60 was required to be in the militia and this duty was taken very seriously by the authorities as well as the settlers themselves, especially in Canada and Louisiana.
The governor could order some or all of the militiamen to be mobilized. The militia was at that time far more than the colony's armed forces reserve; it was also its police force and it performed a myriad of civilian activities from firefighting and fire prevention to conducting censuses. The fighting spearhead part of the militia was made up of men who were used to life in the wilderness, the *coureurs des bois* and the *voyageurs*, canoe men who conducted trade with the Indians right to the very edges of the known world. These men, who had to have great physical strength and endurance for such a life, were outstanding woodsmen who were very adept in the uses of muskets, tomahawks, and hunting knives. From their

dealings with the Indians, many of them knew their languages and were intimately familiar with their customs.

Indeed, the majority of the Indian nations, after some conflicts in the 17th century, were won over by French diplomacy that articulated a mixture of kind gestures, such as gifts, backed up by strong military actions. From the 1690s, the French had developed tactics that could seek out and humble almost any native opponents in the farthest and most remote points of the wilderness while also cajoling them to be trade partners rather than go on fighting. Many Indian nations had already opted for friendly relations, and in a historic meeting held at Montreal in 1701 that brought together hundreds of delegates from Indian nations with the governor-general and his officials, the "Great Peace" was proclaimed. This diplomatic triumph was in many ways a series of alliances and it lasted to the very last years of the Seven Years' War. The few, such as the Fox nation, who were opposed to the French and their Indian allies, were annihilated. Even some of the Mohawk Iroquois, traditional enemies of the French since 1609, were attracted; a number of them moved to the Montreal area, where their descendants still dwell. As noted above, the French lavished gifts on the Indians and worked hard to create good personal links with them. For instance, there was an officer cadet establishment in both Canada and Louisiana, and part of the training of many of these future officers featured a residence of many months at an allied Indian village to learn the nation's language and culture.

Following the 1754 Jumonville incident, the French colonies in Canada and Isle Royale (now Cape Breton Island in Nova Scotia) were seen by officials in Versailles as being the most threatened by British and American forces. Thus between 1755 and 1757 eight French line infantry battalions were sent to Canada and two to Louisbourg, the capital of Isle Royale, with a total of about 6,000 officers and men – 7,450 when one includes two battalions sent to Louisbourg in 1758 as well as a few replacements. Suffice it to say here that only 3,310 went back to France. None of these troops were involved at the Ohio Valley frontier. The only regulars there were those of the Compagnies Franches de la Marine, detached mostly from Canada but with strong contingents coming from the Illinois Country in Louisiana. Militiamen also came primarily from Canada with smaller parties being from the Illinois settlements.

Since the 1680s, officers in Canada had pondered on the best ways to conduct warfare in the North American environment. Population was sparse, distances enormous, winters long and harsh. There were hardly any roads so nearly all transport was done on the rivers and lakes that acted as highways in the summers. European tactical Art of War manuals were useless in this new land because they were intended for armies fighting in Europe. Cavalry or numerous trains of siege artillery could not be deployed on a land-based campaign in North America. As a result, there were no mounted troops in Canada and gunner detachments remained in fortress cities such as Quebec. On the other hand, the officers observed that Indians, and also many Canadians involved in the fur trade, moved rapidly by canoe in summer and

Eastern woodland Indians, mid-18th century. On the left, a fully equipped warrior in summer dress. At center, a chief wearing a European-style hat, coat, and waistcoat, as well as a gorget; all items that were gifts from French and/or British officials. On the right, a warrior dressed for colder weather with a hooded "capot" coat. (Reconstitution by David Rickman. Collection and photo: Directorate of History and Heritage, Department of National Defence, Ottawa)

would even make long winter journeys through the wilderness using snowshoes. The tactics used by the Indians were correctly observed to be outstanding for their shock and surprise factors, but the French also knew that Indian warriors could fight fiercely or totally change their humor and decide to go home on a whim.

Canadian officers from the Hertel and the Le Moyne families along with officers from France felt that a form of *petite guerre* (small war), which was carried out by partisans and Hungarian hussars in Europe, might be adapted to local circumstances and should be tried out in North America. In 1686 a party of French soldiers and Canadian militiamen led by the Chevalier de Troyes and Pierre Le Moyne d'Iberville mounted a hitherto incredible winter expedition that went from Montreal to the shores of Hudson Bay and proceeded to raid and take the competing English fur trade forts established there. Not only was the booty rewarding, but it signaled that such operations – as far-fetched as they were – could be carried out with great success. It was as if the wilderness had become akin to an ocean where raiders, much like corsairs, could roam at will and strike without warning. Furthermore, those who volunteered could be recompensed by booty. Yet, far from being piratical ventures, these raids could be well organized with a cadre of experienced regular officers and a core of soldiers and Canadians used to the wilderness. Allied Indians obviously saw the potential because they were soon added to the composition of raiding parties, but would always remain an independent entity. They usually collaborated with the instruction given by French officers during attacks, but could not be restrained from leaving at any moment. This was followed by many more "French and Indian" expeditions against the enemies of New France that terrorized the western borders of the English colonies in the decades to come. By the middle of the 18th century, the French and their Indian allies were the nearly undisputed masters of the wilderness thanks to these tactics. Few Americans from the British seaboard colonies dared to venture into the forests to the west.

Possession of the Ohio Valley became a contested point between Britain and France. The French based their claims on the explorations of Robert Cavelier La Salle during the previous century, while the British claimed that it was part of Iroquois country, and since the Iroquois were British subjects, the land belonged to them. As time passed, the number of American traders in the region increased steadily. The governor-general of New France became alarmed, and, in 1749, sent some 30 soldiers and 180 militiamen, accompanied by a few Indians from Montreal to the Ohio under the command of Captain Céloron de Blainville, an experienced frontier officer. Along the way, they buried lead plates to indicate that this territory belonged to the king of France. A few years went by and, from the French point of view, the situation worsened. The Marquis de Duquesne was sent from France as governor-general with instructions to secure the Ohio Valley for France. He sent Captain Paul Marin de la Malgue, accompanied by 300 infantrymen of the Compagnies Franches de la Marine, 18 gunners of the Canonniers-Bombardiers, about 1,200 Canadian militiamen, and 200 allied Indians to secure the whole area. Fort de la Presqu'île (now Erie, Pennsylvania) on the southern shore of Lake

Erie was completed in May 1753, and Fort Le Boeuf in July. Then a detachment proceeded to the confluence of the Allegheny and French rivers and began the construction of Fort Machault at the Indian village of Venango (today Franklin, Pennsylvania).

Meanwhile, the governor of the British colony of Virginia, Robert Dinwiddie, was equally convinced that the Ohio Valley belonged to the king of England, and would not tolerate the new French forts. He sent an ultimatum to Fort Le Boeuf, demanding that its garrison leave the area. The young man bearing this message would one day become world famous: George Washington. The ultimatum did not impress either Captain Saint-Pierre, who received it on December 11, 1753, or Governor-General Duquesne in Quebec City. Instead, Duquesne sent a large expedition on February 3, 1754 to reinforce the Ohio. Arriving on April 16 at the junction of the Monongahela and Allegheny rivers, the French troops found a company of Virginian soldiers building a fort and ordered them to withdraw, which they did the next day. The French soldiers then built their own fort, which they named Fort Duquesne (today Pittsburgh, Pennsylvania) in honor of the governor-general of New France. By its strategic location, Fort Duquesne was the key to the Ohio Valley. For the French, it had a great importance because they could communicate faster with Louisiana by using, from Lake Erie, the Allegheny River, which, when it met the Monongahela River, formed the mighty Ohio that flowed west all the way into the Mississippi River, just south of the French settlements in the Illinois Country. There were other waterways further west to reach the Mississippi River, but this one was of utmost importance. Strategically, the French authorities felt that if it was not secured, an enemy force could come up to Lake Erie and cut off their communications between east and west on the southern Great Lakes. It would also render tremendous harm to their prestige with the Indian nations of the Ohio Valley and the Great Lakes.

For his part, Governor Dinwiddie was not about to be cowed by the French occupation and proposed energetic countermeasures: the construction of a fort on the shores of the Monongahela River, the mobilization of some 800 militiamen, and the immediate raising of a provincial corps of 300 volunteers. The French simply could not be left in possession of the Ohio Valley. Not only did it block the American colonists and traders from going further west, but in wartime the French would surely use their forts as bases to mount expeditions against Virginia, Pennsylvania, and Maryland. Another factor complicating the situation was that Virginia's neighboring colony of Pennsylvania was governed at the time by Quakers, a pacifist religious sect. It was thus the only American colony not to have a law obliging men to serve in the militia. However, Virginia was a large, prosperous colony with some 27,000 militiamen on its muster rolls. From February 1754 its legislative assembly approved the measures proposed by Dinwiddie and the Virginia Regiment was formed, and a detachment was sent to the Ohio under the command of the young Colonel George Washington. However, on the morning of May 28, 1754, Washington's detachment of 400 Americans and their Indian allies made a surprise attack on a French negotiating party of

Americans surveying land beyond the Blue Ridge Mountains toward the Ohio Valley in the late 1740s. Indians look on, wondering what is going on and sometimes reporting these activities to the French. Print after JOB in the 1914 *Washington: Man of Action*. (Author's photo)

MAY 28 1754

Jumonville Glen; start of fighting in the Ohio Valley

about 40 men under the command of Ensign Joseph Coulon de Villiers, Sieur de Jumonville. Within 15 minutes, ten men were killed, including Jumonville, and only a Canadian militiaman named Monceau succeeded in escaping and returning to Fort Duquesne. On June 26, Captain Louis Coulon de Villiers arrived at Fort Duquesne with reinforcements and learned of the death of Jumonville, who was his brother. Now with sufficient forces and eager for retribution, Coulon de Villiers went after Washington and his men, and soon found them huddled in their own hurriedly built Fort Necessity at Great Meadows (near Farmington, Pennsylvania). After a heavy exchange of fire, which killed about a hundred Americans, Washington capitulated. The repercussions of these events created a diplomatic storm in Europe, which led to war between Britain and France.

Unlike New France, the British seaboard colonies had few regular soldiers. In 1754 the largest contingent was in Nova Scotia, where the 40th, 45th, and 47th regiments were posted, to a total of approximately 1,500

Colonel George Washington, Virginia Regiment. Although this 19th-century painting shows the regiment's officer's coat buttons and lace as being of gold, they were actually silver. (Unknown artist. Collection and photo: Fort Ligonier Museum, Ligonier, Pennsylvania)

officers and men. The rest of the colonies had barely 550 regular soldiers of the British colonial independent companies posted in New York and South Carolina. Even when adding the few artillery detachments and a hundred rangers in Nova Scotia, there were only about 2,300 men and officers of all ranks. With the exception of the rangers, these troops also knew nothing about the art of war in the wilderness.

The local government of the British American colonies was very different from that of New France. Because each colony had been settled for different reasons, often by groups of colonists who had left Great Britain because of religious persecutions, the political link with the mother country was more tenuous. Thus, largely left to themselves, Puritan settlers in Massachusetts, Catholics in Maryland, and pacifist Quakers in Pennsylvania, along with enterprising planters in Virginia and traders in New York, had built, practically on their own, prosperous and well-managed overseas provinces that flew the flag of Great Britain. They were governed by their own elected legislative assemblies presided over by a governor appointed by the British crown. Because of the substantial powers enjoyed by the various American legislatures, the best royal governors were those who worked well with both the London government and the local politicians. In matters of defense, for instance, local legislatures could vote for funds to raise and maintain their own "provincial" troops that might serve for about six months a year during the warm season, which they usually did at times of emergencies or during hostilities. Otherwise, security was mostly insured by militiamen called on duty for a short period of time.

In the 1754 British American colonies, exasperation reached a peak following the battle of Fort Necessity. Virginia decided to raise its own small army, while North Carolina, New York, Connecticut, and Massachusetts were preparing to follow its lead to deal with the "French and Indian" crisis. American politicians unanimously demanded that regular troops from the British army be sent to North America at once. Now thoroughly aroused and giving in to American pressures, the British government authorized the funds to raise two regular regiments, the 50th and the 51st, each to have a thousand men recruited in the North American colonies. To deal with the immediate crisis on the Ohio, the government ordered the 44th and 48th regiments with an artillery detachment to sail for Virginia. The 1,500-man expedition, which was under the command of Major-General Edward Braddock, who was appointed commander-in-chief in North America, landed in mid-March of 1755.

The British strategy, assuming there was one, appears to have consisted of taking the French outpost forts. With the help of the American troops, Braddock and his regiments were to occupy the Ohio Valley, while those stationed in Nova Scotia were to take the French outposts on the isthmus of Chignectou. Other ventures such as attacking Fort Saint-Frédéric on Lake Champlain and Fort Niagara on Lake Ontario were mooted. All this was to occur during peacetime; an official state of war had not yet been declared between Britain and France. When the French court heard that British troops were on their way to Virginia, six line infantry battalions were hastily ordered to Quebec and Louisbourg. The British fleet failed to intercept these troops, while the regiments in Nova Scotia went on the offensive and easily took the French forts of Beauséjour and Gaspereaux in June.

With this success, things looked promising for the main offensive: General Braddock's army's march to take Fort Duquesne. The key to settling the question of who was entitled to the Ohio was about to be settled by the 2,200 British regulars and American provincial troops that were heading towards the French fort; progress was slow because they had to build a road through the wilderness. By July 9, 1755 they had crossed the Monongahela River and were only about 12 miles (20 km) from the French fort. They advanced with drums beating, when the vanguard began to fire into the woods where a detachment of 105 officers and men of the Compagnies Franches de la Marine, with 146 Canadian militiamen, and more than 600 Indians ambushed them, fanning all around the Anglo-American force which was soon decimated by their deadly fire. The French and Indians were well hidden in the forest and made frightening Amerindian war cries. Confusion was followed by panic and then flight. The Anglo-American army lost 977 men, of whom some 500 were killed, including General Braddock, who fell mortally wounded, while the French had minimal losses: only 23 killed and 16 wounded. From the standpoint of the Canadian officers of the French colonial troops, the victory was undeniable proof that their tactics could vanquish both American militiamen and British regular troops from Europe.

Quite apart from the fact that the Ohio Valley was definitely off limits to any British or American advance, the Indian nations were even more encouraged to mount countless small raids that set ablaze settlements in the western parts of Virginia, Maryland, and Pennsylvania. Furthermore, many Americans became terrified of the hostile Indians because of the horrible fate suffered by many of those that fell into their hands. In that part of the American colonies, the tables had turned and the French in Canada tried to keep the initiative to maintain the British and Americans on the defensive. Perhaps as an afterthought, war was formally declared between England and France on May 18, 1756, nearly two years after fighting had broken out in the Ohio Valley.

That year, Britain ordered the four-battalion 60th Regiment raised in America, and sent the 35th and 42nd regiments over to North America, while France sent two more army battalions with the talented General Montcalm as commander. He quickly proceeded to take the heavily fortified position of Oswego on the shores of Lake Ontario. The following year was not very encouraging for the British and Americans. This time, Montcalm came down lakes Champlain and George, and took Fort William-Henry in July 1757, while the planned expedition on Louisbourg was aborted due to a strong French navy squadron cruising in its area. As for the Ohio Valley, nothing further had happened there.

Things were, however, about to change for the British. Since December 1756, the new British government led by William Pitt changed the manner in which the war was being fought. Pitt convinced his colleagues and King George II that the wealth and glory of Britain was to be found overseas, not in Europe. Insofar as New France was concerned, there could only be one solution: large-scale invasion. Britain already enjoyed naval superiority. Thus, Britain's war effort shifted overseas, while France's armies became increasingly committed in Germany. With its allies, the empires of Austria and Russia, France expected to easily overwhelm the kingdom of Prussia allied to Britain. For France, the European war had started out quite well with the 1756 capture of the British fortress island of Minorca in the Mediterranean, while French armies were gaining ground in Germany and by the summer of 1757 had occupied Hanover, which was then a British territory. Nevertheless, the kingdom of Prussia was proving far more resilient than anyone expected in spite of being attacked simultaneously on all sides. Its king, Frederick II, proved to be one of the most outstanding generals of modern times and he outfought the allied armies. On November 5, 1757 the French were crushed by Frederick at Rossbach, which led to their

The battle of the Monongahela, July 9, 1755. It was a disastrous defeat for the British and American troops as they neared Fort Duquesne, inflicted by a much smaller force of French soldiers, Canadian militiamen, and Indian warriors. In the foreground, young Colonel George Washington of the Virginia Regiment attempts in vain to rally fleeing soldiers. Commanding Major-General Edward Braddock was mortally wounded in the encounter. Print after JOB in the 1914 *Washington: Man of Action*. Author's photo.

MAY 18 1756

Declaration of war between France and England

evacuation of Hanover. This disaster forced the French government to send more troops to the German front, where they were met with further defeats. Consequently, France's overseas empire was neglected. No substantial reinforcements were sent to Canada thereafter.

The American colonies meanwhile greeted a steady flow of reinforcements arriving from Britain, such as the 17th, 77th, and 78th (the latter two both Highland) regiments in 1757. The following year the 15th, 28th, 58th, and 62nd line infantry regiments, as well as more gunners, joined the army already in place. In addition, a light infantry regiment, the 80th, was raised, bringing the regular British army in North America to approximately 23,000 men. American troops raised in the various "provinces" and serving full-time from the spring to the late fall of each year represented another 22,000 officers and men in the field during 1758. Additional to these provincial troops were about 200,000 American colonial

Skirmish in Hampshire County, West Virginia, Spring 1756. In the early part of the war, the French, Canadians, and their allied Indians prevailed on the frontier. However, the Colonial Americans did have the occasional success against these raiders. In the spring of 1756, Virginia Militia Captain Jeremiah Smith of Albemarle County arrived in Hampshire County, Virginia, then on the western edge of settlement and today part of West Virginia. He was just in time: "...a party of about 50 Indians, with a French captain at their head, crossed the Allegheny Mountains... Capt. Smith raised a party of twenty brave men, marched to meet this...foe, and fell in with them at the head of the Capon River, when a fierce and bloody battle was fought. Smith killed the captain with his own hand; five other Indians have fallen...they gave way and fled." Episodes such as this were repeated scores of times in the frontier counties of what is now West Virginia, which also supplied recruits for the full-time Virginia Regiment. (Painting by Jackson Walker. Collection and photo: US National Guard Heritage Series)

militiamen listed in the muster rolls. Some of these were occasionally called upon for guard duties and in emergencies. No accurate figure is known as to how many mustered, but it is certain that their numbers dwarfed the New France militiamen called on duty because of the huge difference in population in favor of the American colonies. By then the French had only about 7,000 regulars to defend Canada and Louisbourg.

INITIAL STRATEGY

The army that went on campaign in Pennsylvania led by Brigadier-General John Forbes was one of three large Anglo-American armies that advanced on various fronts during 1758. This was the result of a master strategic plan conceived during 1756–57 by John Campbell, Earl of Loudoun, who had been commander-in-chief of the British forces in North America before his recall to England in December 1757. Lord Loudoun, who had served in the entourage of the royal family, had a talent for strategic planning as proven by his plan to invade New France. When he arrived, he inherited the sequels of Major-General Edward Braddock's July 1755 disaster at Monongahela, the stalemate on the Lake George–Lake Champlain front, and some timid progress on the western frontier of Nova Scotia that was now ravaged by some formerly neutral Acadians that had escaped an unwarranted deportation and exacted their revenge. Indeed, it seemed the frontier was aflame everywhere due to innumerable "French & Indian" raids. Actually mostly Indian raids because many native nations perceived the French as being uninterested in large-scale settlement, while it was obvious to most of them that if the Anglo-Americans came, most Indians would lose everything.

John Campbell, Earl of Loudoun, c.1753. During his tenure as commander-in-chief in North America during 1756 and 1757, General Loudoun formulated the master strategy that was followed by the British government for the conquest of New France. He is shown in the uniform of the 30th Regiment of Foot. (Collection and photo: Fort Ligonier, Pennsylvania)

Finding there was no coherent Anglo-American war plan, Lord Loudoun conceived an invasion strategy for the conquest of Canada that would

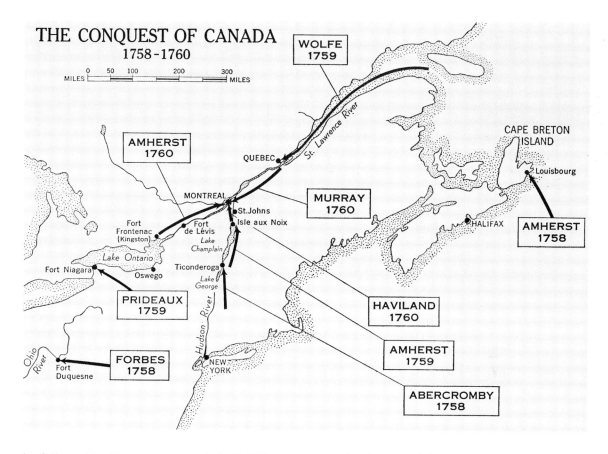

THE CONQUEST OF CANADA
1758-1760

WOLFE 1759

AMHERST 1760

CAPE BRETON ISLAND

Louisbourg

QUEBEC

MONTREAL

MURRAY 1760

HALIFAX

AMHERST 1758

Fort Frontenac (Kingston)

Fort de Lévis

St.Johns

Isle aux Noix

Lake Champlain

Lake Ontario

Fort Niagara

Oswego

Ticonderoga

Lake George

PRIDEAUX 1759

Hudson River

HAVILAND 1760

AMHERST 1759

Ohio River

Fort Duquesne

FORBES 1758

NEW YORK

ABERCROMBY 1758

St. Lawrence River

be followed by his successors and the British government for the rest of the war. This strategy called for overwhelming forces to be deployed on three fronts: the Ohio Valley, the Lake George–Lake Champlain–Richelieu River area towards Montreal, and the Fortress of Louisbourg on Isle Royale (Cape Breton Island), which would lead to the St. Lawrence River and Quebec. The final objective was Montreal, where all three armies were to meet. Loudoun had correctly perceived that it was Montreal, and not Quebec, that was the real strategic and commercial key to New France. This grand strategy called for the capture, amongst other objectives, of Fort Duquesne to secure the Ohio Valley, and thus allow the British and American forces to move up to Lake Erie and, eventually, Lake Ontario.

The missing element of the British and American war plans was the question of the Indian nations. General Braddock's 1755 defeat on the Monongahela had made it abundantly clear that there could be no sustainable penetration in the hinterland without a dramatic shift in policy regarding Indians. For generations the French had lavished considerable effort and money to sustain a diplomatic stance towards the Indian nations that brought them either their alliance or at least their neutrality. The result was that, apart from a few recalcitrant nations, the French held sway through their allies in North America's hinterland to the very edges of the forests that bordered the British colonies. There was one large exception to this situation on the outskirts of the colony of New York: the League of the Six Nations making

Strategic map of the conquest of Canada, 1758–60; Lord Loudoun's grand strategic plan was carried out over three years. In 1758 two of the year's three objectives fell: Fortress Louisbourg in July and Fort Duquesne in November. They were repulsed at Fort Carillon (Ticonderoga), but took it the following year along with Quebec and Niagara. In 1760 three armies marched on the ultimate objective, Montreal, where the French army capitulated on September 8. (Collection and photo: Directorate of History and Heritage, Department of National Defence, Ottawa)

JANUARY
1757

77th
Highlanders
raised

up the Iroquois Confederacy. These were the Mohawk, Oneida, Onondaga, Cayuga, Seneca, and Tuscarora nations. The sixth and most recent nation was the Tuscarora, which had been at war with and defeated by North Carolina settlers in the early 18th century, moved north, and been adopted into the league. The original five nations had come together to create the confederacy in about 1570 and had spent much of the next century launching devastating hostilities on French-allied nations, such as the Hurons, as well as on the French settlements and outposts. Somewhat let down by the English when the French mastered the art of wilderness warfare in the 1690s, they adopted a more neutral position. However, most Iroquois, especially the original five nations, remained attached to Great Britain. Those among them that had more sympathies for the French had moved to live in the area around Montreal. Thus, the majority who remained in what is now upstate New York favored allegiance to the British "King George" and hoped for more attention from his officials. This came in 1755 with the appointment to the new post of Superintendent of Indian Affairs of a most talented Englishmen that lived in their midst: William Johnson. He was gifted with outstanding diplomatic ability as well as a good understanding of military command, which he had promptly displayed by rallying the Iroquois and, in September 1755, defeating a French metropolitan regular force that attacked an American provincial army at Lake George, even capturing its wounded French general, Baron Dieskau. For these amazing feats, he was knighted.

Sir William went on to many more successes during the war in the northern areas. But the superintendent had little influence, if any, on Indian nations in the Ohio Valley and its surrounding areas. This was the domain of the western Delaware (called the *Loups* – Wolves – by the French), Shawnee, and Mingo nations. In turn, they had welcomed and often fought alongside many warriors that had come from further west and the Great Lakes belonging to the Ottawa, Wyandot, and other nations allied to the French that had set up their camps near Fort Duquesne.

If the British and Americans were to have a chance to succeed in regaining the Ohio, their Indian diplomacy would need a great deal more attention, something that Sir William Johnson could not effectively give, not only because he was much too preoccupied in the north, but also due to his connection with the Iroquois, which did not necessarily endear him to most Ohio and Great Lakes nations. During 1756 and 1757, Indian diplomacy in the Ohio, while all-important to the French, was not a great priority to the British and Americans, who were then preoccupied on other fronts and busy mustering as many troops and warlike stores as possible to implement the great strategic plan devised by Lord Loudoun. Following this plan, an Anglo-American army would march into the Ohio to secure Fort Duquesne. No one wanted a repetition of the disaster on the Monongahela, and for that not to happen, quite apart from a new tactical approach, there also needed to be concerted and massive efforts to neutralize the Ohio Indian nations at the very least.

In London, Prime Minister William Pitt defined the command structure of the Anglo-American forces and their objectives for the following year in

MARCH 14
1758

General Forbes
ordered to
Philadelphia

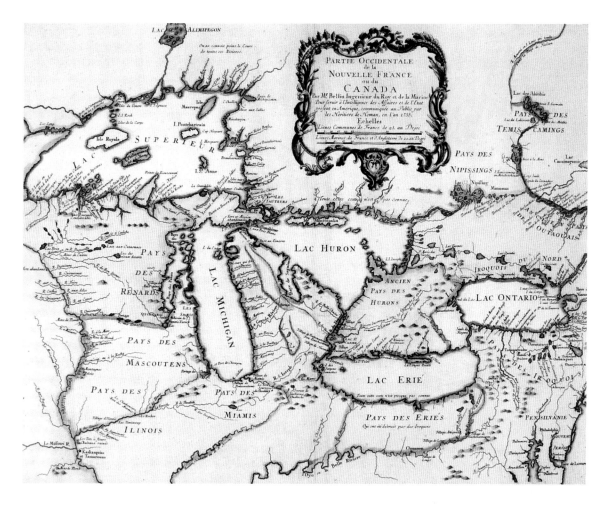

a letter dated December 30, 1757 and received at New York on March 4, 1758. In terms of command, Sir James Abercromby replaced Lord Loudoun as commander-in-chief in North America. In 1758, imperial strategy would be exerted on three fronts. The most important in terms of military and naval resources would be an attack on the Fortress of Louisbourg by a large British fleet of more than 150 ships manned by 14,000 sailors and marines under the command of Admiral Boscawen, and transporting some 13,000 British regular soldiers led by Major-General Jeffery Amherst.

Meanwhile, Sir James Abercromby would advance up Lake George and take Fort Carillon at Ticonderoga and Fort Saint-Frédéric (Crown Point, New York) on the southern shore of Lake Champlain, leading an army of some 17,600 men of which nearly 6,000 were British regulars.

The third front consisted of an advance across Pennsylvania to expel the French from the Ohio. The force gathered to achieve this goal was to be smaller – about 6,500 men, of whom nearly 5,000 were American provincial troops, and the remainder British regulars.

In terms of the strength of the French forces they were to face, all three Anglo-American armies had greatly superior numbers of troops compared to those of their respective opponents. There was, however, a sizable

Territorial map of the Indian nations in the Great Lakes and Ohio Valley regions in the 1740s and early 1750s. Except for the almost annihilated "Renards" (Fox) nation at left, the various nations were either French allies or neutral. The data was compiled for years before the map was actually drawn up in Paris by cartographer Bellin and "communicated to the public" in 1755. (Library and Archives Canada, NMC 192944)

Lieutenant-General Sir James Abercromby, *c.*1755. He was commander-in-chief in North America during 1758. (Collection and photo: Fort Ligonier Museum, Ligonier, Pennsylvania)

difference between the projected Ohio Valley campaign and the two others. In the case of moving upon Ticonderoga and Louisbourg, it was expected that the French would have several thousand regulars as defenders, and that, especially for Louisbourg, trains of siege artillery would be required and probably a European-style assault by lines of British troops on fortified positions. In the Ohio, the operation consisted really of a very long-distance raid by a very strong force on a very weak but strategically all-important position made almost impregnable by its very remoteness in the wilderness.

To command the smaller army that would strike towards the Ohio, Prime Minister Pitt selected Colonel John Forbes, commander of the 17th Regiment of Foot already in Halifax, Nova Scotia. The 17th stayed in Halifax as part of the army intended to attack Louisbourg, but its colonel was promoted to brigadier-general and instructed on March 14 by General Abercromby to go to Philadelphia and organize his new army. Forbes had been born in Edinburgh, Scotland on September 5, 1707 and entered the army aged 22 as a surgeon in the 2nd Royal North British Dragoons, also known as the Scots Greys, later becoming a subaltern officer. By 1744 he was a captain and had been at the battle of Dettingen, Germany the previous year. He would again see action at Fontenoy in 1745 and Lawfeld in 1747. Obviously a bright and

hard-working officer, he was noticed by senior commanders and became an aide-de-camp to Sir John Campbell. Then, in December 1745, he was promoted deputy quartermaster-general of the British cavalry in the Duke of Cumberland's army in Germany with the rank of lieutenant-colonel. In that function he gained valuable administrative experience that would later serve him well in Pennsylvania. After the end of the Austrian Succession War in 1748, he went back to Scotland and became lieutenant-colonel of his old regiment, the Scots Greys, and colonel of the 17th Regiment of Foot in February 1757. At that time Forbes was still a bachelor, but he was starting to experience some problems with his health. Nevertheless, his administrative experience was sought in North America and he soon joined Lord Loudoun in New York as adjutant-general.

Forbes was now one of the key officers on the staff of the commander-in-chief for North America, where he was perceived as competent enough to be recommended to the prime minister for higher command. Pitt, no doubt feeling there would be a great deal of administrative work in preparing the army to move on to the Ohio, wisely selected Forbes, who had management skills as well as experience in battle. One aspect unknown to everyone, however, was Forbes' health – as months passed, he seemed to suffer more and more frequently from a digestive ailment.

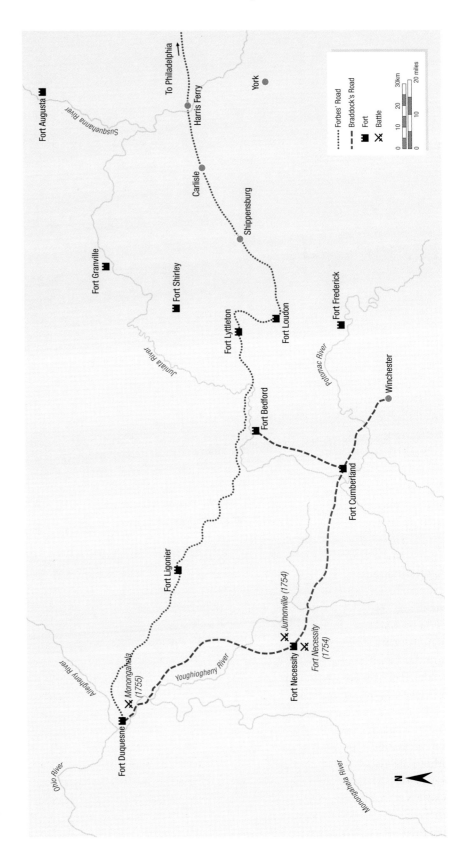

The routes of Braddock's and
Forbes' Roads.

THE PLAN

On April 18, 1758 the newly promoted brigadier-general arrived in Philadelphia. Elsewhere, the armies under Abercromby and Amherst were already formed. In the case of Forbes' command, it consisted only of himself and a few staff officers; everything else had to be organized. As adjutant-general, Forbes had encountered many army officers and he now selected several of them whose talents would be especially suited to organizing and providing senior command to his army. As his second in command, Forbes called upon Henry Bouquet, the Swiss-born lieutenant-colonel of the 60th Regiment's 1st Battalion. In early 1758 he was the military commander at Charleston, South Carolina, from whence he reported to his new duties in Philadelphia in mid-May. He also had campaign experience in European battlefields and had served in the Sardinian (also called Piedmontese) and Dutch armies before joining the British army in 1755 to participate in organizing the new 60th (Royal American) Regiment. The army's brigade major was Captain Francis Halkett, detached from the 44th Regiment, whose father had been killed nearly three years earlier at the battle of the Monongahela. Captain Halkett had served as General Braddock's brigade major during that unfortunate campaign. Thus, he was familiar with the terrain and the challenges the wilderness offered. The quartermaster-general selected by General Forbes was Lieutenant-Colonel Sir John St. Clair of the 60th Regiment, an officer that was experienced in staff duties involving logistics because he had previously been deputy quartermaster-general in other commands. He had campaigned in Flanders during the 1740s, had arrived in Virginia during 1755, and was also a veteran of the Monongahela. These were the senior staff officers of Forbes' army who would plan the campaign and, like their general, all were efficient and experienced career officers.

Lieutenant-Colonel Henry Bouquet, c.1755. He was the senior officer after General Forbes in his army during the 1758 campaign. (Print from an unsigned portrait. Author's photo)

To make up the bulk of the army, 14 companies from two British regular regiments, three American provincial regiments with smaller detachments of infantry as well as artillery, and a company of light cavalry were assigned to the force.

Of the British regiments, four companies of the 60th (Royal Americans) Regiment's 1st Battalion totaling 16 officers and 406 non-commissioned-officers (NCOs) and other ranks were transferred from South Carolina to Philadelphia. The 60th was a peculiar unit in the army, being more like a "Foreign Legion" than a British unit. For one thing, it had a strength of four battalions instead of a single one like other British line infantry regiments, and it was, at least initially, mainly recruited from German and Swiss soldiers in Europe. Both countries were renowned for the quality of their soldiers and many European nations had "foreign" establishments within their armies, made up mainly of German and Swiss regiments. Their soldiers traditionally kept to themselves as a group, and often only understood German unless they were from a French-speaking canton in Switzerland. The German and Swiss officers, however, were fluent in French and that was their language of choice as is proven by Colonel Bouquet's correspondence with General Forbes, who, like all senior and well-educated British officers, also knew French. The 60th Regiment's American recruits were hoped to be immigrant settlers of German origin in Pennsylvania (the so-called Pennsylvania "Dutch" that were not from Holland but eventually often passed as such because "Deutch" – meaning German in that language – became altered to "Dutch" in English). Soon, however, recruits from anywhere were welcome.

The other British line infantry unit was very different, being a gathering of Scots from the Highlands. It was raised from January 1757 by the Honourable Archibald Montgomery who "mixed much with the people, and being a high-spirited young man, with a considerable dash of romantic enthusiasm in his composition, and with manners cheerful and affable, he made himself highly acceptable to the Highlanders; and by the support which he met with, and the judicious selection of officers of influence in the North [of Scotland], he soon completed an excellent body of men," according to Stewart of Garth. After being posted in Charleston, South Carolina, for a few months – where some of the men became sick and some died due to the unfamiliar warmer climate – the 77th Montgomery's Highlanders was

Lieutenant-Colonel Sir John St. Clair, quartermaster-general of Forbes' army in 1758. He is wearing the uniform of the 60th Regiment: a scarlet coat with dark blue lapels and small collar tab, and silver buttons. (Print from a miniature by J.S. Copley. Author's photo)

transferred to Philadelphia, where, in early June 1758, it mustered 41 officers and 1,059 NCOs and privates. Three new companies were added to the ten previously raised, making some 1,250 men by July 11. Its appearance must have been highly conspicuous in the Quaker city. Officers and men wore Highland clothing that included the dark-blue bonnet, the belted plaid that formed both an ample shoulder sash and a skirt-like kilt, and checkered stockings. And they were armed with large Scottish Claymore swords and iron pistols as well as the usual muskets and bayonets. Not only were they a sight to behold, but, like it or not, since the regiment had many pipers, the sound of bagpipes might be heard even before they came into view. Nor was it necessarily easy to converse with some common soldiers as many of them only spoke Gaelic although they could understand drill orders in English.

Thus Forbes had, in effect, two somewhat un-English regular infantry regiments as far as their composition was concerned, with some of the men not having a working knowledge of English. This, however, was not a great obstacle because for any formal maneuvers, all knew the English command words. Much more worrisome to Forbes and his senior officers was the obvious fact that the great majority of his regulars had never been in combat, and thus were professional soldiers but "green" insofar as battle experience. Some older NCOs might have seen smoke and bullets during "The Forty-Five" in Scotland, or the campaigns in Germany during the 1740s, but, even for these men, the prospect of a firefight in the middle of the wilderness against seasoned woodsmen and screaming Indians must not have been too reassuring, especially in view of Braddock's disaster three years earlier.

The other detachment of regulars was much smaller, but very important. It consisted of two officers and 35 artillerymen of the Royal Artillery assisted by a dozen civilian artisan employees of the Board of Ordnance, the government body that supervised artillery and engineering as well as the supply of small arms and ammunition in the British forces at that time. These troops arrived in Philadelphia with a very substantial train of artillery that included 18 brass light 24-pdr cannons, 16 brass light 12-pdrs, 14 brass light 6-pdrs, four 3-pdrs, and eight brass howitzers and 38 brass mortars of various calibers. One notes that the recently introduced new brass light cannons had been selected, no doubt because all knew that Forbes' army would be moving through difficult terrain. In that sense, a light 24-pdr weighed less than a ton, while a heavy 24-pdr was about 3 tons. With these came a thousand muskets and a hundred carbines with an immense quantity of flints, powder, tools, barrels, and every sort of supplies needed for an army about to enter a campaign.

Nevertheless, General Forbes felt it was too much artillery to drag across the Pennsylvania wilderness. Such a huge train would likely result in many delays, and he questioned the wisdom of bringing the "light" 24-pdr cannons at all over such a terrain on a very long distance that included crossing a mountain range. Just the barrel of such a brass light cannon could weigh up to 1,800 pounds. This was without its carriage, made of heavy hardwood reinforced with forged iron, which increased its weight further. The prospect of having artillery pieces weighing over a ton traveling on a muddy back

Private of a battalion company of the 60th (Royal American) Regiment, c.1757–60. The uniform had blue facings; unlike for other infantry regiments, the privates' and corporals' uniforms were not laced. (Watercolor by Derek FitzJames. Collection and photo: National Historic Sites, Parks Canada)

road was dubious to say the least in America's wilderness. The general therefore cut down the ordnance accompanying the army to:

- 6 brass light 12-pdr cannons
- 8 brass light 6-pdr cannons
- 2 brass 8-inch howitzers
- 2 brass 5½-inch howitzers
- 1 brass 8-inch mortar
- 2 brass 5½-inch mortars
- 12 brass 4 2/5-inch (Coehorn) mortars

It was still a respectable total that should prove sufficient to reduce Fort Duquesne to ashes. The rest of the cannons, howitzers, and mortars were left in Philadelphia, the heavier pieces such as the 24-pdrs being mounted on the shores of the Delaware River to deter any French ship that might venture in the area. Philadelphia was not fortified and had no citadel, but it had the large Association and Society Hill shore batteries to protect its harbor.

The Board of Ordnance did not send along engineers with all this artillery material. Yet Forbes had to have engineers if his army was to progress through the Allegheny Mountains to reach Fort Duquesne. Because there were never enough Royal Engineer officers available, it was common practice to detach regimental officers skilled in military engineering to perform these duties, usually under the supervision of a Royal Engineer officer. In the case of Forbes' army, there was none assigned. This was most likely because the Ohio campaign was not likely to involve complicated siege operations. The building of country roads, frontier forts, and elementary siege batteries and trenches did not require a fully fledged Royal Engineer officer, whose talents were required to tackle Louisbourg or West Indian citadels. One of Colonel Bouquet's junior officers in the 60th Regiment, Ensign Charles Rhor, turned out to have the required skills in engineering and he was accordingly appointed chief engineer by General Forbes, who also appointed several other officers to assist him.

For the bulk of his army, General Forbes would have to depend on American provincial troops. These were not professional soldiers like in the regular British army and those mentioned above. British soldiers were enlisted for life, or at least for the length of a war, after which they might be disbanded. American provincial soldiers were enlisted for a season, and might never enlist again the next year. Although there seem to be no overall figures as to whether many private soldiers reenlisted in provincial battalions year after year between 1755 and 1763 in North America, it seems that a fair proportion of NCOs and officers did. Through these years of service, many

Regimental color of the 60th (Royal American) Regiment, c.1757–60. (Reconstitution. Fort Pitt Museum, Pittsburgh, Pennsylvania. Author's photo)

of them acquired a military experience that could equal if not surpass that of the more junior officers and men of the regular British army. This appears to have been the case with regards to the army led by General Forbes. In this regard, the part of the provincial American contingent that came from Virginia undoubtedly had many officers and men that had previously been in action against the French and Indians on the western frontier. Some, like Colonel George Washington, were even veterans of the terrible defeat on the Monongahela in July 1755. However, the composition of these troops was very diverse and while there might have been seasoned fronticrsmen amongst them, many others would have been from cities or farms, and those coming from Pennsylvania's three Lower Counties, which are now the state of Delaware, were more familiar with the seashore than the primeval forest they were about to march into. In one of his more discouraged moments, Forbes felt provincial soldiers were, except for some of their officers, an "extremely bad collection of broken innkeepers, horse jockeys and Indian traders," forgetting that Americans, when they did soldiers' duties, had a very different attitude toward army life than Europeans. This was a temporary occupation to defend their communities in times of emergency, not a permanent way of making a living.

Therefore, soldiering for an American in the middle of the 18th century was simply not a career choice. There was no colonial American regular army to enlist in, and it appears that very few men were interested in signing

A British brass light 12-pounder cannon on its carriage, 1750s. This was the largest type of gun brought by the army that marched towards Fort Duquesne. (Reproduction. Fort Ligonier Museum, Ligonier, Pennsylvania. Author's photo)

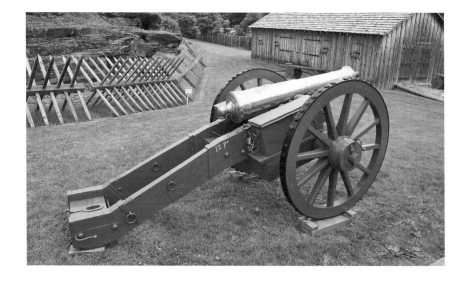

their lives away for a red coat and a shilling a day in the British army. This was as true for enlisted men as it was for officers. Apart from a few exceptions, American gentlemen were not especially attracted to a career in the regular army, even if some of them could afford to buy commissions. They came from a different community, which they and their ancestors had built, and often held different views on society and its values than those of their counterparts in England. So they acknowledged the authority of British officers to command and of British politicians to direct imperial policy during the Seven Years' War, despite many grudges, thanks to the common goal of winning the war. In the case of General Forbes, Colonel Bouquet and other British officers in Pennsylvania, the Americans were fortunate in having intelligent and generally open-minded men to liaise with talented individuals such as Washington or Benjamin Franklin.

Ammunition wagon, mid-18th century. This type of wagon was drawn by four horses and had a capacity to carry up to 1,200 pounds. "Ammunition" at the time could include various types of military stores, tools and rations. (Reproduction. Fort Ligonier Museum, Ligonier, Pennsylvania. Author's photo)

Probably the most valuable provincial contingent came from Virginia and it formed nearly half of the provincial forces in Forbes' army. It consisted of the 1st and 2nd Virginia regiments under the command of colonels George Washington and William Byrd respectively. In July 1758 both regiments mustered 2,004 officers and enlisted men. Colonel Byrd was 58 years old and had much experience on the frontier as well as with relations with Indian nations. But it was Colonel Washington who, in spite of his youth, had more experience and knowledge of the Ohio than anyone else in the army, since he had roamed that area first as a surveyor, then as Governor Dinwiddie's messenger, and finally as a military officer. His Virginia Regiment, numbered 1st in March 1758 when the 2nd Virginia Regiment was raised, dated back to 1754 and by 1758 appears to have had a strong regimental tradition. Its detachments had seen action with the Jumonville incident, at Fort Necessity, the Monongahela, and many frontier skirmishes. Many of its officers and men seem to have reenlisted from year to year for the usual five to six months of service. Well led and trained, and fairly well equipped, it was arguably one of the finest provincial units in the American colonies. When Colonel St. Clair inspected several companies of the 1st Virginia in May 1758, he reported to Forbes that he was impressed by what he had seen and that fine services could be expected from this unit. Colonel Byrd's 2nd Virginia was being recruited and organized with a cadre transferred from the 1st Virginia, but St. Clair was also pleased by the men that he saw, while quite angry about the fact that many had not yet received their weapons and both regiments were also short of tents and many other supplies that were stored in Philadelphia. Eventually, everyone got their weapons, supplies, and uniforms, which in the case of the Virginia regiments were dark blue with red facings, silver buttons, and lace decorating those of the officers. Perhaps to mark the distinction between them as American soldiers and the "Redcoats" of the British army, the provincial soldiers

Small mortar and powder carts, mid-18th century. The small brass Coehorn mortars would have been transported on this type of sturdy cart. The long carts in the background contained four barrels of powder in its central locker, which was covered with waterproof oilcloth. The two lockers on each side held spare shots and shells. (Reproduction. Fort Ligonier Museum, Ligonier, Pennsylvania. Author's photo)

usually tended to have blue or green uniforms for their infantry units rather than red, although there were exceptions.

Although the Pennsylvania Quaker population was still demographically important and politically powerful, waves of settlers of other beliefs and origin had also put down roots and prospered in the province. These settlers were not as pacifist as the Quakers and clamored to have some military organization. At the behest of Benjamin Franklin and other prominent men, volunteer armed associations had been formed in the 1740s and, with warfare erupting on the western frontier in the 1750s, concerned citizens pressured their legislature to provide some military aid. At length, compromises were found and provincial troops were allowed to be raised and funded.

The Pennsylvania contingent for 1758 was quite large by colonial standards and consisted of three numbered battalions forming the Pennsylvania Provincial Regiment. However, the regiment had no central command and actually operated as three separate and distinct units. The 1st Pennsylvania Battalion was commanded by Colonel John Armstrong, a frontiersman who, two years earlier, had led a daring and successful raid on

Brigadier-General John Forbes as colonel of the 17th Foot, c.1757. Colored sketch made at the beginning of the 20th century by the Reverend Percy Sumner of a portrait of the mid-18th century (whereabouts presently unknown). (Sumner notebooks. Anne S.K. Brown Military Collection, Brown University Library, Providence, USA. Author's photo.)

77th (Montgomery's Highlanders) Regiment of Foot, Private, Battalion Company, 1758.

The officers and men of this regiment raised in the Highlands of Scotland in 1757 wore the traditional "garb of our ancestors" that included bonnets, belted plaid (part of which made up the kilt), checkered stockings, and short-skirted jackets. Usually, in the early years of the Seven Years' War, Highland regiments wore jackets without lapels, but the authorities then pressed for them to have lapels like other British regiments. This plate thus shows lapelled jackets because, in December 1759, the Clothing Board of General Officers censured Murray's 42nd and Fraser's 78th for having failed to comply with "His Majesty's Orders", and ordered their commanders to produce new "patterns of a clothing properly laced and lapelled" for the Board (WO 7/26). One notes that the 77th is not mentioned, which indicates that its jackets most likely already had lapels as per the royal orders. A powder horn etching of the period, though a less formal source, also shows a Highland soldier wearing a lapelled jacket. With regards to the tartan used by the 77th for its plaid, Captain John Knox's memoirs mentions an incident involving a soldier of either the 77th or the 78th that was "wrapped up in a dark-coloured plaid" which implies that it was the Government tartan, also worn by the 42nd. Highlanders were armed with the standard army musket with its bayonet, the long-bladed "Claymore" Highland sword (instead of a shorter hanger) and, in addition, Highland pistols and dirks.

French allied Indians camped at Kitanning north of Fort Duquesne on the shore of the Alleghany River. The 2nd Pennsylvania Battalion was led by Colonel James Burd, who had engineering and military experience as well as being gifted with social skills that granted him influence in the colony's political structure; this proved to be an asset. The 3rd Pennsylvania was led by Colonel Hugh Mercer, who had been a surgeon in "Bonnie Prince Charlie's" Jacobite army during 1745–46 before emigrating to America where he also distinguished himself at Kitanning. All in all, these were men with good experience who were likely to make effective field commanders during the campaign. The enlisted men from Pennsylvania were from varied backgrounds, although there seems to have been a high proportion of former indentured servants. The recruits were somewhat hampered as new soldiers because they had not even been exposed to the yearly militia musters and so had only a very sketchy idea of the most basic elements in a military organization. There were few qualified sergeants to drill them so training was, at least initially, a huge challenge. Nevertheless, some 2,276 officers and men made up the three battalions, which was quite a respectable total for a nominally pacifist province. In addition, there were three provincial infantry companies from the Lower Counties (now Delaware).

The colony of Pennsylvania also had a small provincial train of artillery further inland at Lancaster, consisting of four brass 6-pdr cannons and two brass 5½-inch "Royal" mortars served by 57 officers and gunners led by Captain-Lieutenant David Hay. Furthermore, a troop of 50 Pennsylvania provincial light cavalrymen was attached to the army.

Pennsylvania provincials as well as those from the Delaware Lower Counties had a green uniform faced with red, as well as, from May 31, 1758, green jackets lapelled "with the same" color. The cavalrymen appear to have had the all-green uniform jacket with a green cloak, buckskin breeches, spatterdashes (gaiters), and a leather cap. The scouts detached from provincial units also wore a "yellow band around the forehead, and a stream-like band of the same color around the arm" to be recognized by allied Indians.

Other colonies provided smaller contingents. Maryland sent a small battalion of four companies totaling 276 officers and men, while North Carolina provided a company of 52 officers and men. The Marylanders may have worn red coats with black cuffs and the North Carolina men were perhaps in blue, but both contingents were badly equipped and clothed, and eventually had to be issued other supplies.

The total number of troops could and did vary. On the whole, Forbes could count on about six to seven thousand effective men to advance against Fort Duquesne. Therefore, by June and July Forbes had the first element necessary for his action plan: a viable army to carry it out. But campaigning in the wilds of North America required another big trump card: either the alliance or at least the neutrality of the major Indian nations in the area where the army would be operating. Considering the fiasco on the Monongahela three years earlier with the first attempt to take Fort Duquesne, this was an essential factor for any Anglo-American force moving toward the Ohio.

Initially, Indian diplomacy was not very successful and the Anglo-American army had to ask for Cherokee and Catawba Indians further south to consider joining the force. Forbes found the Cherokees to be very reluctant in spite of gifts and promises. However, by mid-May about five or six hundred Cherokee and Catawba warriors were heading for Pennsylvania to join Forbes' army. Meanwhile, Pennsylvania politicians had tried to open a dialogue with the Indian nations, and, in 1757, a treaty with the Delaware Indians had been agreed to at a meeting at Easton (New Jersey); another gathering was mooted sometime in 1758.

News from elsewhere was not very encouraging. On July 8, General Abercromby's attack on Fort Carillon at Ticonderoga was beaten back by General Montcalm's French army; the desperate charges by British regulars on the French positions had failed and resulted in very high casualties. Abercromby had felt compelled to withdraw. Thus, one of the three assaults on New France had failed and it was the one that involved the largest Anglo-American force led by no less than the commander-in-chief in North America. To make things even worse, hundreds of Iroquois warriors attached to Abercromby's army had watched the fiasco at Ticonderoga and word of it soon reached the other nations.

Some weeks previously, pacifist Pennsylvania merchant Israel Pemberton, who had founded the Friendly Association for Regaining and Preserving Peace with the Indians by Pacific Measures, came on the scene of native diplomacy urging the Indians to hear what the Pennsylvania authorities would have to say when considering their allegiances. Forbes immediately saw an opportunity and asked General Abercromby to negotiate directly with the Indians. To his credit, the general transferred the responsibility of Indian Affairs in the Ohio from Sir William Johnson to General Forbes on July 23. Johnson was of course upset but, to his credit, Forbes immediately sensed the importance of what turned out to be a momentous decision and exploited it fully. Less potent in Pennsylvania, but also important, was the news that on July 26 the French Fortress of Louisbourg had fallen to General Amherst's army. This was, at last, positive news to inform the Indians about the might of the British forces. Another meeting was called at Easton in October; it was months away, but suddenly the Anglo-Americans had something to offer, and thus upset the diplomatic upper hand the French had always enjoyed.

Meanwhile, General Forbes had to choose a route over which the army would travel to its objective: Fort Duquesne. There was already General Braddock's road that had been built from Winchester, Maryland, in 1755 and which, with some repairs, would get the army to within a dozen miles of the French fort. The most obvious problem with this road was that the French and Indians likely expected the Anglo-American army to come by that route. They would keep it under close surveillance and undoubtedly set up ambushes and raids. There was also another reason that had to do with logistics. The Braddock Road started out further south. Virginia and Maryland, as General Braddock had found out, were not especially well provided with wagons, animals, and supplies that far in the wilderness.

Pennsylvania was much better in that respect and Forbes, who rightly considered that the operation depended crucially on good logistic support, decided to stay in that province.

There was another possibility: the Old Trading Path used by Indians and fur traders that went right across western Pennsylvania. It started at Harris Ferry on the Susquehanna River and progressed west through the Alleghany Mountains to the headwaters of the Ohio River where Fort Duquesne stood. It would have the advantage of good logistical support thanks to ample means of transportation that were available in Pennsylvania. A stretch of the trail called Burd's Road, going west up to Raystown (later Fort Bedford), had been substantially improved by James Burd and his men in 1755. From there, as Bouquet put it to Forbes on June 21, it was "shorter, avoiding all the rivers, having only small creeks to be crossed." Although not a military factor, building a large road out of the trading path would certainly encourage trade and settlement more than Braddock's Road after the war. Finally, it might, according to Bouquet, even "confuse the enemy who naturally would not expect us from that direction" since the French would most likely assume that the Anglo-American army would come by Braddock's Road, which was indeed the case (Bouquet, II: p. 123).

By the end of May, Forbes had made up his mind and opted to use the route through Pennsylvania. The possibility that French and Indian war parties might come east by using Braddock's Road to outflank his force was quite remote. Besides the huge distances involved, two major obstacles would deter any raiders: Fort Cumberland and, a short distance to the east, stone-walled Fort Frederick were more than a match for any raiding party. The risk of flanking movements by enemy raiding parties north of the chosen Pennsylvania route was even more remote; there were no major trails and no sizable waterways east of the Alleghany River until one came upon the Juanita River and, even further east, the Susquehanna River, and both rivers had forts on their shores to intercept hostile traffic. Therefore, until the Anglo-American army would pass the Juanita River at Raystown, it was a relatively safe road upon which to tread. This too must have been comforting to Forbes and his senior officers.

Broadly, the plan was to build the road methodically and advance cautiously towards Fort Duquesne. The distance between Philadelphia and the French fort was about 450 miles (750 km), but serious road-building would really occur past the Susquehanna River to make Burd's Road more passable. After Raystown, the trail would have to be rebuilt into a real road and that would have to pass the Alleghany Mountains, the Laurel hills, and the Crescent ridges before finally approaching the low hills that were just to the east of Fort Duquesne. At all times the army had to be as safe as could be, which required camps to always be well guarded along the way. Furthermore, larger permanent fortifications would be necessary as staging areas when the army approached its objective. In many ways, Forbes and his officers were taking a leaf from Caesar's *Commentarii de Bello Gallico* and Vegetius' *De Re Militari*, both well known as the 18th century witnessed a massive interest in ancient Roman and Greek antiquities. For military officers, especially those of senior ranks, the study of such classics was expected, and copies would likely be among their baggage. The principle outlined by the Roman writers was the safety of the army when it penetrated deeply into the largely unknown territories of barbarian enemies. It applied admirably to the operation that was about to get under way. More modern writers were often inspired by the ancient texts, and Forbes mentioned having been especially influenced by the 1754 *Essai sur l'art de la guerre* by French military theorist Count Turpin de Crissé, one of the more popular manuals of the time. This hussar officer's account was translated into English by Captain Otway, but Forbes appears to have used the original French edition. In any event, he later wrote to William Pitt that he had applied "the Generall principles upon which I have proceeded" from Turpin "regarding precautions by having posts along my route..." (CO 5/50).

From late April, but especially during May, contingents gradually moved westward towards Raystown, 217 miles (349 km) from Philadelphia, where all units would regroup. Also heading there were up to 360 supply wagons as well the artillery. Forbes instructed Bouquet to go ahead to Raystown while he remained at Philadelphia with St. Clair to sort out various supply problems, then headed out in late June. Meanwhile, as he moved west, Bouquet found the existing road increasingly difficult and finally found it easier to built an entirely new one west of Fort Loudoun, and reached Fort Lyttleton (also spelled Littleton), which had been built by Pennsylvania

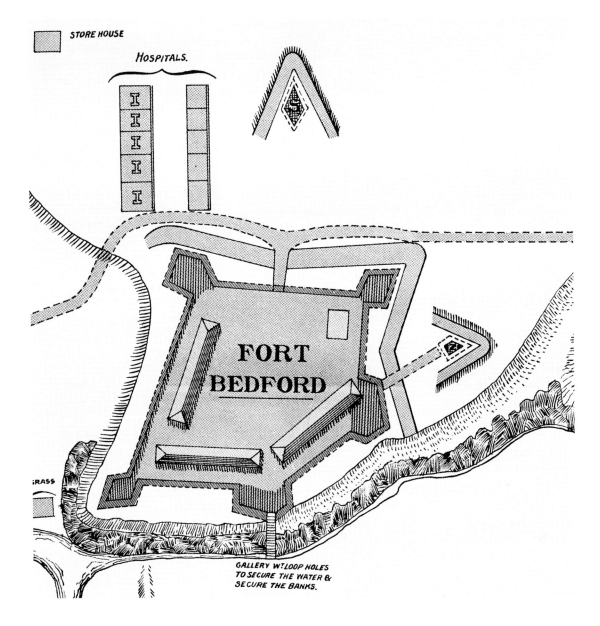

provincials two years before. As Bouquet and his men progressed further, they had to negotiate small hills that required reverse curves and 90-degree turns in the new road, which soon became known as Forbes Road. At last, in mid-June, the Juanita River was reached and work on a small fort started that was nearly finished by June 23.

The troops and supplies continued to arrive at what was called Fort Bedford. Additional field fortifications were erected by units as they arrived so that proper protection would be in place. By early July, Forbes himself reached Fort Bedford and the growing fortified camp around it. Up to that point, the army's march had been through relatively safe and geographically passable territory. Forbes and his senior officers were, once again, faced with the question as to which way to go. The army could still opt to take Braddock's Road by marching south to Fort Cumberland because the prospect of crossing the Alleghany Mountains raised fears that it might not be possible to actually build the road through this range. Bouquet favored due west by going through the mountains, but it was Forbes who was responsible and would have to answer to London for the feasibility of the operations. Bouquet was well aware of this and, before proceeding further, he sent four scouting parties to evaluate again the obstacles ahead, namely the Alleghany Mountains and, further on, the Laurel Hills.

The most critical account regarding this route was that submitted by Chief Engineer Rhor who, while stating that a road through the Alleghany Mountains could "not be cut for waggons without a Immense Labour" for at least three-quarters of a mile on a "very steep" incline, he went on to report that about two miles to the east-northeast of the "Old Trading path" was a gap he had found that was "very narrow with a gradual ascent & stony, but with a good deal of Labour a Road might be cut" (Cubbison: p. 87). The three other scouting parties were led by captains Colby Chew of the 1st Virginia Regiment, Asher Clayton of the 2nd Pennsylvania Battalion, and Edward Ward of the 1st Pennsylvania Battalion, each of whom had been given very detailed instructions from Bouquet when they set out on July 7. Each party came back with reports describing what they had seen regarding the obstacles ahead. By the end of July, Bouquet could report that "avec beaucoup de travail on pourroit y pratiquer un Chemin beaucoup plus facile que l'autre" (Bouquet, II: p. 288, translated as: "with a great deal of work a road much more satisfactory than the other could be built there" in Bouquet, II: p. 291; but "facile" is far better translated as "easy" rather than "satisfactory" which is "satisfaisant" and gives a more lukewarm approbation. Bouquet's strong opinion, crucial at this point of the projected raid, is much better expressed in his native French language). Quartermaster General St. Clair also agreed with Bouquet because the road due west would provide plenty of fodder for the many bullocks and horses necessary to pull the wagons and artillery of the army, which was not to be found in necessary quantity by using Braddock's Road. Having to bring the animal's food over such a distance was likely to create a logistical and financial nightmare.

After viewing all these options, General Forbes leaned toward the continuation of the road due west through the gap found. However, his

OPPOSITE: Plan of Fort Bedford, 1758. This fort was built at Raystown (Pennsylvania) because it was designated the main assembly point for General Forbes' army. It was an irregular pentagon of picketed curtain walls with five corner bastions and an 8-foot (2.4 m) deep ditch outside. A couple of outside redoubts were built northwest (right) and southwest (top) of the fort. A branch of the Juanita River was nearby (bottom). The great majority of the 7,000 soldiers assembled at that site camped outside the fort. Buildings such as the hospital and store houses were built outside its walls to accommodate these troops until August when the army marched west. A small garrison was left at the fort, which provided safety for many nearby settlers from Pontiac's Indians in 1763. It was abandoned thereafter. (Print from T.C. Montgomery's 1916 *Frontier Forts of Pennsylvania*. Author's photo)

decision was not quite made when a serious case of insubordination by a senior officer occurred in early August. Not everyone agreed and, no doubt fed by rumors, young Colonel Washington, the senior of the American provincial commanders, still felt that Braddock's road was the better option. Hearing this Colonel Bouquet confronted him at a meeting and reported to Forbes that Washington had given him "rien de satisfaisant" (nothing satisfactory) regarding ways to overcome the problems with Braddock's Road (Bouquet, II: p. 288). But Washington was stubborn and made his feelings known by letters to Colonel Halkett and to the Governor of Virginia. Somehow, General Forbes quickly learned of this and Washington was now in trouble with his commander-in-chief, who felt it was a "shame" to see "any officer" participate in the opponent's "Scheme against this new road" westward. On August 11, Forbes reported to his own commander-in-chief, General Abercromby, that he had let it be known "Very Roundly" to Washington and his acolytes "that their Judging and determining of my actions and intentions before I had communicated my opinion to them was so premature, and was taking the lead in so ridiculous a way that could by no means suffer it." (Forbes, pp. 171, 173). As a result of pulling political cards to undermine his general, Washington found himself very much discredited by his commander-in-chief, the senior British officers, and also the Pennsylvania provincial officers who favored the western road through the mountain gap. For the first time in his career Washington had played and

A view of Fort Bedford's northwest side, summer of 1758. As can be seen in this painting by Nat Youngblood, there is a lot of activity outside of the fort. (Fort Pitt Museum, Pittsburg. Author's photo)

There are no known portraits of Lignery and Aubry, so this rendering of a senior officer of the Compagnies Franches de la Marine in his dress uniform, reaching for a pinch of snuff, illustrates these officers. He wears the medal of a knight of the Order of Saint Louis hanging on a scarlet silk ribbon awarded to Lignery in 1755 and to Aubry in 1760. (Watercolor by Eugène Lelièpvre. Collection and photo: National Historic Sites, Parks Canada)

British and American troops, ordnance, ammunition, and supply wagons moving on Forbes Road, built across Pennsylvania during the summer and fall of 1758. (Painting by Nat Youngblood. Fort Pitt Museum, Pittsburg. Author's photo.)

lost, keeping only the support of his fellow Virginians. And it could be argued that his foolish act of insubordination not only caused General Forbes to humble him, but, most of all, to definitely opt for the road west from Fort Bedford.

While all these events were going on in the slowly advancing Anglo-American army, the French flag flew high over Fort Duquesne. General Forbes and Colonel Bouquet were having much difficulty in obtaining accurate intelligence about the strength of the French and of their Indian allies, and also the actual warlike state of the fort itself as well as its associated fortifications. For various reasons, it seemed to be considered next to suicidal for Anglo-American scouts or rangers to actually approach near enough to spy on the fort and get back alive to report viable information on the French position. In spite of that, a few lone forays had been made such as Captain Chew's August scout who came back with a pretty useless sketch of the fort (missing two bastions!) along with equally dubious information on its garrison observed from far distant hills. Therefore, information on the strength of the French and Indian force came from Indians' hearsay, the few British or Americans that had escaped Indian captivity, and French deserters – who were even fewer – all of which were not especially trustworthy. That this was a persistent problem is abundantly clear in General Forbes' letters. As late as September 21, he reported to General Abercromby that, according to American Indian trader George Croghan and interpreter Andrew

**FORBES ROAD
THE CLEAR FIELDS**

Good forage found at open camps such as this on the Raystown Path, led General Forbes to prefer this route to Braddock's Road. Site of Fort Dudgeon (Tomahawk Camp) is a short distance to the north.

PENNSYLVANIA HISTORICAL AND MUSEUM COMMISSION 2005 ©

Forbes Road today. Pennsylvania Highway 30 basically follows the road built by the British and American forces in 1758. The area shown is between Bedford and Ligonier. The Pennsylvania Historical and Museum Commission plaque reads: "The Clear Fields. Good forage found at open camps such as this on the Raystown Path, led General Forbes to prefer this route to Braddock's Road. Site of Fort Dudgeon (Tomahawk Camp) is a short distance to the north." (Author's photo)

Montour, the "Enemy's strength both as to Indians, French and Canadians and the present situation of their fort be infinitely stronger than any thing I ever could have imagined... [Croghan and Montour] sending me positive accounts that their numbers exceed greatly 4000, in and about the Fort..." By October 8, Croghan was still insisting that there were about 4,000 enemies, but Forbes now informed Abercromby that "This I cannot believe" and now thought that "their whole force are not more than 1200 men which is in their fort..." A week later, on October 15, Forbes wrote to Bouquet informing him that the Ohio Indians had told the participants at the meeting going on in Easton at the time that "the French will have in those parts near four thousand men French, Canadians, & Indians. That they have provisions in plenty as yet; That the Canadians are not at all in the Fort but that they as well as the western Indians were scattered about in the Indian villages where they help the inhabitants to build huts & houses and were ready at a Call" (Forbes: pp. 217, 227, 230). Thus plagued with obviously dubious information, General Forbes was rightly suspicious about American intelligence services.

On the French side, everyone knew in Fort Duquesne that major reinforcements amounting to thousands of troops would not be coming to the Ohio Valley to face a large Anglo-American army. The defense resources of New France were already stretched to the limit and its few thousands of regular soldiers could be concentrated on only one front. In the summer of

Officer-cadet and sergeant, Compagnies Franches de la Marine, Canada, 1750s. Both of these men are dressed in the regulation-issue uniform usually worn in the settled areas and, possibly, only on parade days in frontier forts. Officer-cadets, most of whom were born in Canada, had the same uniform, arms, and equipment as private soldiers, but with a blue and white aiguillette at the shoulder. Besides the arms training (shown here) and academic training, they could also be detached to an allied Indian nation to learn native languages and culture before obtaining their regular officer's commission in the French colonial troops. Sergeants had gold lace edging on the cuffs and pocket flaps, and carried halberds in the more formal duties in towns, or muskets otherwise. (Watercolor by Eugène Lelièpvre. Collection and photo: National Historic Sites, Parks Canada)

Compagnies Franches de la Marine, wilderness outposts, 1730s to 1750s

In frontier areas such as the Ohio Valley, officers and men took to wearing Canadian dress, consisting of a hooded capot, mitasses, breechclouts, and moccasins, saving their European style uniforms for more formal occasions. The short-skirted mild season style capot is shown here as the most likely to have been worn in the late summer and fall of 1758. This very handy garment widely worn by French settlers in New France as their ordinary dress was, for soldiers, probably made from the cloth of their older issue European-style military issue uniforms. Hence the predominant colors would have been grey-white or blue. Capots did not have buttons down the front and were instead fastened by a waist sash, or a belt, or both. The Indian-style leggings, or "mitasses", tended to be mostly made from sturdy woolen material of various colors. Forage caps were also made from old uniforms and could have been grey-white with a blue turnup as shown, or all blue, etc. Beards, and facial hair in general, were frowned upon in both European and Indian societies so the men were most likely clean-shaven, even on the frontier. The soldiers carried a standard Model 1728 military issue musket with bayonet. Unlike the French Metropolitan army since the late 1730s, soldiers of the colonial Compagnies Franches carried cartridge boxes at the waist rather than the shoulder. In the wilderness, they replaced their swords with the more versatile tomahawk, and also carried knives like the Canadian militiamen. Indeed, much of their costume and equipment made them resemble Canadian fur traders, and made them very well-suited to carry out bush warfare.

1758, most of the French regular troops were grouped south of Lake Champlain to face General Abercromby's army that was heading for Fort Carillon at Ticonderoga. Small numbers of colonial regulars and militiamen would be sent to hold other areas in the hope that a major enemy force would not show up. In the case of Fort Duquesne, possibly the most important reinforcement came not from Canada, but from the French outposts in Illinois, also called Upper Louisiana. This area was part of the colony of Louisiana and had its own garrison of about 300 or 400 men of the colonial Compagnies Franches de la Marine regulars. Since Illinois was not threatened, Commandant Macarty detached part of its garrison and some Illinois militiamen in several large bateaux to Fort Duquesne where they arrived in July according to J.C.B. This party of about 240 men was under the command of Captain Charles-Philippe Aubry, one of Louisiana's best officers. His presence there would prove to be a thorn in the side of Forbes' Anglo-American army.

In 1758, the commander at Fort Duquesne was François-Marie Marchand de Lignery. Born into a Montreal military family on August 24, 1703, he became an officer-cadet at age 14, was commissioned second ensign on April 1, 1733, lieutenant on April 17, 1744, and captain on April 1, 1751, the highest rank that could be achieved in the colonial Compagnies Franches de la Marine. He participated in major frontier campaigns as early as 1728 against the Fox Indians, later in Louisiana against the Chikasaws in 1739–40, in Nova Scotia in 1745–46, and was later posted in the Ohio. He played a leading role under Captain Dumas during the battle of the Monongahela in July 1755 that resulted in Braddock's defeat and death. By then, he was a seasoned and experienced frontier officer. Temporary appointments as area commandants were possible for further promotion and Lignery was selected in early 1756 to command Fort Duquesne, which made him the senior officer in the Ohio. He was made a knight of the Order of Saint-Louis on March 17, 1756 in recognition for his excellent record of service throughout his military career.

Lignery's challenges were immense. He was in charge of a weak force guarding an area that the French high command had decided to abandon, should a large enemy army move against it. If he had read such manuals on the defense and attack of fortified places, he knew that none of Marshall Vauban's precepts would be of any use for his fort at the head of the Ohio River. Chances are that he had as Montreal probate records show that Canadian officers could be as well read as their French and British counterparts, and possibly better than their commissioned American adversaries, because nearly all the leading military literature was published in French. But nothing in those manuals addressed the sorts of issues they had to cope with on the North American frontier. For that, they relied on the unwritten Canadian wilderness warfare doctrine practiced since the 1680s. It was ideal against a powerful and numerous enemy, as would be Spanish guerrilla tactics half a century later, but it had its limits. Those limits seemed to have been reached when news that a large army of several thousand men equipped with artillery had Fort Duquesne as an objective. For one thing, although good intelligence was just as difficult to get in the

French camp, it was a foregone conclusion that the enemy force would be a much larger army than Braddock's, and that it would move cautiously so as to avoid another Monongahela-like disaster.

The reinforcements that had come from Illinois also brought Captain Charles-Philippe Aubry, who turned out to be ideally suited to serve in the Ohio in 1758. Born in about 1720 in France, he entered the army when 14 years old as a second lieutenant and campaigned in Germany, Bohemia (now the Czech Republic), and Italy during the 1740s. Seeking promotion and adventure, he joined the Louisiana colonial troops with the rank of captain in 1750 and by the mid-1750s was in Illinois. Obviously fascinated by its natural environment and its Indians, he quickly mastered the precepts of wilderness warfare and, as an experienced and competent career officer, was soon second to Illinois Commandant Macarty. In 1757 he founded what would become Fort Massac on the Ohio River near the Mississippi and the following year arrived at Fort Duquesne. There, he was second in command. Competent and in the prime of life, Aubry most probably had an engaging personality combined with strong leadership qualities. He must have infused new optimism to Commandant Lignery and his garrison as soon as he arrived.

The numbers of men, both French and Indian, that Lignery could count on fluctuated and could not be high because of the limits to the supplies that could be transported to the Ohio. Rations for the 4,000 men reported by Croghan were simply unrealistic. No musters appear to have survived, but at most, during the summer of 1758, there might have been up to between 700 and perhaps as many as 1,000 French soldiers and Canadian militiamen in the Ohio. According to artilleryman and occasional Fort Duquesne storekeeper J.C.B., 180 men arrived from Montreal to reinforce the fort's garrison in March and another 240 with Captain Aubry in July. Commissary General Doreil mentioned in July that "five hundred men have been sent" but it is uncertain if this included part or all of the above (DCHNY, X: p. 762). There might also have been other much smaller groups arriving. The fort's basic winter garrison strength is unlikely to have been less than 200 men and was possibly somewhat more than that. To this was added a greatly fluctuating number of Indians who also had to be fed and given gifts. These consisted of corn, trade goods, ammunition, the occasional muskets, and some kegs of brandy. Nearly 500 had arrived from the Michilimackinac area in March, and there would have been hundreds more from the Ohio Valley and other areas by the summer. Corn was plentiful but other supplies were not; rations to feed several hundred men would likely start to run out during the fall. A rough calculation of some 186,000 daily rations for officers, soldiers, militiamen, and Indians issued at Fort Duquesne between June and November show that they peaked in August and September with some 42,600 and 45,000 monthly rations issued respectively, which come to a maximum of about 1,500 rations daily in September. Some of these would have gone to allied Indians, who also consumed corn and bear's grease as well as some fresh meat, notably 20 dogs in September. The number of soldiers, militiamen, and Indians was reduced from October because rations

**SEPTEMBER 14
1758**

**Grant's raid on
Fort Duquesne**

issued now fell to 960 a day and down to 760 a day in November (as related in: *Papiers Contrecoeur*: pp. 429–431).

The fort itself was considered indefensible and pretty rickety. Montcalm wrote to the minister of war in Versailles that "Fort Duquesne is good for nothing and is falling." Commissary General Doreil also observed that Lignery was unfortunate in having such a command, because the fort was "fit only to dishonor the officer who would be entrusted with its defense" and was sure to tarnish his reputation. It was obvious that the structure was next to worthless if subjected to an artillery bombardment and assault by a large enemy force; in such a case, Lignery "had orders to burn [the fort] and to [previously] remove the artillery, warlike stores and provisions on the approach of the enemy" and evacuate the garrison to other forts (DCHNY, X: p. 922).

But before all that, there might be some opportunities to "tickle" the Anglo-American army by harassing it with raids. In May, Lignery had reported that the "English Indians" had "killed one of his garrison." As a result "his Indians had avenged him by bringing him 140 prisoners or scalps, and he has still more than 100 Indians in the field in different parties." From the prisoners, he learned that "the English desire to come and besiege Fort Duquesne with a force of 4,000 men; there is every disposition to receive them well" (DCHNY, X: p. 841). However, the rumored enemy army did not seem to be approaching. Not much was known about it and there was no tangible sign of it by August. Reports going back to Quebec kept saying that "everything is quiet" in the Monongahela River area. The Anglo-Americans were naturally expected to come by Braddock's Road, the only existing roadway, so the scouting parties were watching that area and, so far, not seeing much...

GRANT'S RAID ON FORT DUQUESNE

Meanwhile, Forbes' army was slowly progressing from Fort Bedford to the next area selected as a major base, a place called Loyalhanna (also called Loyal Hannon or still Royalhanna and spelled several ways). In early August Colonel Bouquet was moving ahead through some very difficult terrain with the spearhead of the army numbering at least 1,500 men with hundreds more required to assist on the road construction. By September 7, he reached Loyalhanna and started setting up a fortified camp. Being in that area was not necessarily a safe proposition. Within a few days of the arrival of Bouquet with the army's vanguard, small parties of enemy Indians were lurking about with, possibly, some Canadians with them also. Several isolated men were attacked and several killed. An alarmed Bouquet wrote to Forbes that he was "surrounded by Indian [war] parties" and detached about 200 men to guard the access to his camp (Bouquet, II: p. 513). Amazingly, for the French and Indians there, this contact with an

Fort Duquesne – the objective of General Forbes' army in 1758. Model at the Fort Pitt Museum, Pittsburgh, Pennsylvania. (Author's photo)

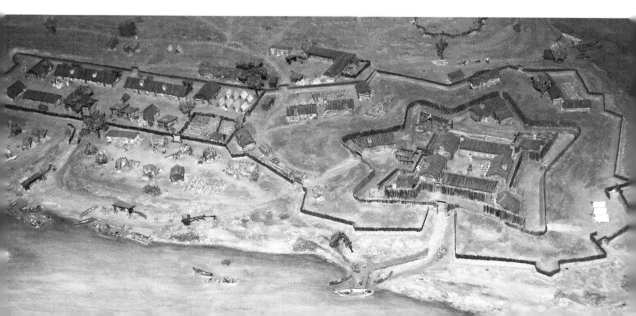

PREVIOUS PAGES:

Major Grant's raid on Fort Duquesne

Having been alerted to the presence of Grant's troops, the garrison at Fort Duquesne formed a strong column under Captain Aubry while Commandant Lignery held a perimeter near the fort. Aubry's column of French soldiers and Canadian militiamen edged the Monongahela River, seemingly unseen by the Anglo-Americans, then turned into the wood covered hills and fell upon the flank of Grant's force. In raid warfare, the best option when attacked is to raid the raiders and that is what these seasoned French and Canadian wilderness fighters did. Firing from behind cover – and the Canadians were renowned marksmen – and rushing in with tomahawks and knives to the sound of fearsome war whoops, the French and Canadians devastated the regular troops who were trained for linear tactics with muskets and bayonets. Their unfamiliarity of the Anglo-American force with this frontier style of warfare is revealed in the huge number of casualties they suffered compared to the few on the French and Canadian side.

Anglo-American detachment does not seem to have registered as being the forward party of Forbes' army. It would appear that, to them, Bouquet's force was just another patrol and the real advance was expected to come from Braddock's Road.

Major Grant of the 77th Highlanders pressed Colonel Bouquet to let him lead a strong party to Fort Duquesne. The idea had earlier been rejected by General Forbes, but Grant did not give up. His concept was to punish the enemy Indians that camped outside the fort where they felt perfectly safe. These were the same Indians that, with encouragement from their French and Canadian allies, plotted raids on the American settlers, villages, and even on isolated parties of regular or provincial troops. This was presently the case with Bouquet's force at Loyalhanna. Such a raid would secure the advance guard better, and correct intelligence about the fort and its garrison would also be gathered. A night attack, something relatively rare at that time, was mooted. Against his better judgment, Bouquet finally agreed. Troops and supplies were trickling in from Fort Bedford every day, so he had enough men to make up a sizable raiding party. In a few days General Forbes would travel from Fort Bedford to the new fort, called Ligonier, that was being built at Loyalhanna. Unfortunately, the general's condition seemed to be worsening and he had to be carried in a litter set up between two horses, but he was still quite sound enough to exercise his command fully. He did not know about Grant's initiative and Bouquet's approval.

The *Pennsylvania Gazette* ran the following account of Grant's expedition: "On Monday 11th of September, Major Grant of the [77th] Highland Regiment, marched from our camp…with 37 officers and 805 privates…" It was actually even stronger, having 860 other ranks. On the 13th they were

within two miles [3.2 km] of Fort Duquesne and left their baggage there, guarded by a captain, a subaltern and fifty men, and marched with the rest of the troops, and arrived at eleven o'clock at night upon a hill, a quarter of a mile from the fort. Major Grant sent two officers and fifty men to the [outskirts of the] fort to attack all the Indians, &c., they should find lying out of the fort; they saw none, nor were they challenged by sentries. As they returned, they set fire to a large storehouse, which was put out as soon as they left it. At day break, Major [Andrew] Lewis was sent with 400 men (Royal Americans and Virginians), to lie in ambush a mile and a half from the main body, on the path on which they left their baggage, imagining the French would send to attack the baggage guard and seize it. Four hundred men were posted along the hill facing the fort, to cover the retreat of Captain McDonald's company, who marched with drums beating towards the fort, in order to draw a party out of the fort, as Major Grant had some reason to believe that there were not above 200 men in the fort, including Indians; but as soon as they heard the drums they sallied out in great numbers, both French and Indians, and fell upon Captain McDonald, and two columns that were posted lower on the hill to receive them. The Highlanders exposed themselves without any cover, and were shot down in great numbers, and soon forced to retreat. The Carolinians, Marylanders, and Lower [Counties] Countrymen, concealing themselves behind trees and the brush, made a good defense; but were overpowered by numbers, and not being supported.

Major Grant was exposed in the midst of the fighting and tried "to rally his men" but to no purpose, as they were by this time flanked on all sides. Major Lewis and his men came up "and engaged [the French and Indians], but were soon obliged to give way, the enemy having the [height] of the hill of him, and flanking him every way." Some were driven "onto the Ohio [River], most of whom were drowned. Major Grant retreated to the baggage, where Captain Bullet was posted with fifty men, and again endeavored to rally the flying soldiers...but all in vain, as the enemy were close at their heels." Attempting to contain the French and Indians, Captain Bullet "attacked very furiously for some time, but not being supported [by other troops], and most of his men killed, he was forced to give way." Major Grant and others were captured, but Captain Bullet made his escape and related that he had last seen Major Grant surrounded on all sides, "but the enemy would not kill him, and often called to him to surrender. The French gave quarter to all that would accept it" (DCHNY, X: pp. 902–903).

This confused attack, seemingly not sticking to a particular plan, was preceded by a night of confusion during which the troops were told to put their shirts over their other clothes to be able to identify friend from foe in the darkness. This was a standard procedure on such occasions. But, for a variety of reasons, there was no attack and certainly no surprise. Miscalculation of the distance, a thick fog, and some parties of the attacking force getting lost in the dark were among the obstacles that prevented the night attack, and the soldiers were now in "the greatest confusion" among Major Lewis' 400 men. The shirts must have come off at dawn. In spite of all that, the raiding force had been incredibly lucky because it still had not been detected by the French and Indians. Instead of calling off the attack, as Bouquet had instructed, Grant now announced to the enemy he was there. Throwing away the advantage of a surprise attack, the Anglo-Americans advanced to the sound of the drums that, in this Pennsylvania wilderness context, must have been as strange as having Indian war whoops at the battle of Rossbach in Europe. The following French accounts relate the ensuing disaster.

On November 1, 1758, the report of Grant's raid by Governor-General Vaudreuil went from Quebec to his superior, the minister of the navy, in Versailles. It collated various reports coming in from the Ohio, some of them undoubtedly verbal. According to this dispatch

on 11 September [1758] Major Legrand [Grant], commanding the Scottish Highlanders that are part of the enemy's army, with 960 men of elite troops...arrived on the 14th in the area of Fort Duquesne. He left 450 men... [in the rear as skirmishers]... and as he planned with the rest of his troops to attack Mr. de Lignery's camp at [Fort Duquesne during the] night by moonlight, he had his soldiers put on white shirts over their clothes for recognition...the watchful guards of Mr. de Lignery having prevented [Grant's troops] from proceeding with his plan, he [Grant] withdrew once he reached the outskirts of the fort.... Major Legrand [Grant], seeing his attack compromised, had the drums beaten to lure the French [garrison] out and charge them, believing them to be a small number. The sound of the drum made the soldiers and the Canadians come out of their tents and huts...all wearing shirts, officers as well as the others, making Indian

GRANT'S RAID ON FORT DUQUESNE

SEPTEMBER 14, 1758

Undetected during its approach, the Anglo-American force announced its presence by setting fire to an outlying building and signaling the advance with pipes and drums. In the fort, the alarm was raised and, within minutes, the defenders assembled. A force under Captain Aubry headed along the bank of the Monongahela, towards the hills occupied by Grant's force, while Commandant Lignery remained with some 200 men at the fort. Once he reached the hills, Aubry's force turned into the woods and fell upon Grant's flank. Meanwhile, Indian allies, most of whom appear to have been camped across the Allegheny, had been also alerted and entered the fight in increasing numbers. The Anglo-American advance slowed then stopped as it was overwhelmed by expert woodsmen in an environment for which it was unprepared. Soon, panic set in and the Anglo-American force broke, with many who could not swim attempting to cross the Monongahela and Grant himself being captured. The raid was an absolute and costly fiasco.

ALLEGHENY RIVER

EVENTS

1   A small Anglo-American forward party sets an outlying shed on fire.

2   The French sound the general alarm and assemble within minutes.

3   Major Grant orders an advance with drums beating and pipes playing.

4   A column of about 500 men under Captain Aubry heads toward the hills, edging the Monongahela River.

5   Approximately 200 men under Commandant Lignery fan out in front of the fort.

6   Aubry's column turns into the wooded hills and falls upon the flank of Grant's force.

7   Indians, most of whom are on the far bank of the Allegheny, cross the river and advance towards the hills.

8   Lignery's men join in the battle.

9   Grant is captured.

shouts… The fight was brisk and stubborn…the loss of the English was 400 killed, a large number wounded and at least 100 made prisoners including the commander [Grant] and other officers. We lost 8 Canadians killed and 8 wounded… Mr. Aubry, captain of the troops of New Orleans as well as all officers of the detachment from the Illinois gave proof of great valor in this affair…[1]

General Montcalm, commander-in-chief of the French forces in Canada, was more concerned with matters closer to the St. Lawrence Valley and the Lake Champlain area, but also was kept informed of events further away. In October his journal included extracts from a September 16 letter from Mr. Du Verny, an "artillery officer detached at Fort Duquesne" regarding Grant's raid. On September 9, Du Verny wrote, intelligence was received that Forbes' army was about "twenty leagues" away and building fortifications there so that scouts were immediately sent out. They came back with the news that the "English army was on the march" but more scouts found that the area seemed to be quiet. They had been looking at the wrong area because on the night of September 13/14 some caught an Englishman who had got lost in the woods looking for strayed horses. Brought back and questioned in Fort Duquesne, he could tell little else to his captors. Nevertheless, here was proof that some enemy force was approaching. At early dawn on the morning of September 14, Du Verny went on

we saw fire in a shed [well outside the fort] and we perceived it had been set by the enemy. A report was made [by the sentries]. A party of 200 men was immediately ordered to make a reconnaissance in the [nearby] woods. As they marched out, at seven in the morning, approaching the woods, they heard many drums and fifes beating, which was also heard in the camp and in the fort. Within six minutes, the French were assembled and headed for the area led by Mr. De Lignery. The action soon began and did not change places. The shooting was very brisk during half an hour; it took much effort to convince the Indians, who were busy ferrying their booty from one shore [of the Ohio River] to another, and I thought I could do nothing better than take their lead and encourage them to join the French who had already gained the advantage [in the battle]. The rout of the enemy was soon complete. We pursued them for three hours. The greater part of this enemy detachment, of about 800 men, was badly mauled or taken prisoner. A small portion swam across the Monongahela River under fire from us and the rest fled in all directions… From that moment, new prisoners were brought every hour of which the greater part fell to the cruelty of the Indians. The commander of this detachment was captured during the fight with several other officers, and many were killed including their engineers. According to the statements of the prisoners, this was merely a detachment of 800 men which had come to reconnoiter and mark [the way to build] a road for an army of seven to eight thousand men that is assembling to come here [at Fort Duquesne] with 18 pieces of artillery.

He added that "we lost ten men, a few wounded; I estimate the loss of the enemy at three or four hundred men." But, Du Verny went on, in spite of this

1 France, Archives Nationales, series K, Monuments historiques, carton 1232, document No. 51

success, "the Indians left us after having made their blow and we were not able to stop them."

Montcalm's aide-de-camp, Louis-Antoine de Bougainville, also mentioned that "a detachment of 800 English, partly regulars, partly militia, had marched very secretly from Pennsylvania…by a very different road from General Braddock's" and "posted themselves at daybreak on a mountain near Fort Duquesne, and made arrangements to facilitate its reconnaissance by an Engineer whom they had brought along. But the troops of the Marine and the Canadians, to the number of 700–800 men, did not give them time. They pounced suddenly from all sides on the English, and immediately threw them into disorder. Our Indians who at first had crossed the river, fearing to be surprised, also charged right vigorously. It was nothing but a route on the part of the enemy. 500 of them have been killed, taken or wounded, and almost all the officers [were also killed or taken]. On our side, only eight men have been killed or wounded" (DCHNY, X: p. 888).

J.C.B. left a short but revealing account of Grant's raid in spite of having been written about four decades after the event. Of those on the French side who left writings of the event, he was, with De Verny, the closest to the action, being in Fort Duquesne as its storekeeper when it occurred. According to his memoir

An army commanded by General Gicent [Major Grant]…had the intention of taking Fort Duquesne by surprise. He consequently had his drums beaten on the shores of the Ohio to lure the [fort's] garrison there, while he was on the shore of the Monongahela River with most of his army to rush on the fort as soon as he would have seen its garrison go away from it. But his plan was foiled. Captain Aubry came out of the fort with about 500 men and, instead of going to where the drums were beating, advanced along the shore of the Monongahela and soon came upon the enemy. The fighting started immediately and was very sharp so that the enemy was put to flight after losing 300 men. Thirty-five prisoners were made including seven by the Indians who gave them to the commandant. The French only had one killed and five wounded, these light losses being because they fought behind trees while the enemy was in the open field.

The commandant of Fort Niagara, Captain Pierre Pouchot, later recalled that on

14 September, 800 Scots and [American] militiamen, under the command of two majors, approached at daybreak right up as far as the cleared ground created around Fort Duquesne, without being spotted. The [American] militia major [Lewis] was hesitant to attack, but the Scotsman, Major Grant, reluctant to turn back without doing anything, had a small shed in an outlying area of the fort set on fire to provoke an engagement. The Canadians [militiamen] and a few Indians, who were lodged in huts around the fort, noted this unusual early morning fire and were curious enough to slide down into the brushwood in order to discover what was happening. They went one after the other. Since the Indians and Canadians wear nothing more than a shirt in fine weather, they were very soon ready for action. Those who arrived first saw the [Anglo-

Regimental color of the 77th (Montgomery's Highland) Regiment, c.1757–60. (Reconstitution. Collection and photo: Fort Ligonier Museum, Ligonier, Pennsylvania)

American] troops and began to fire on them. The English beat the retreat, causing the alert to be sounded in the fort from which assistance was sent to the first men who had sallied forth from it. The enemy corps was so vigorously attacked that 250 scalps resulted and 100 prisoners were taken, among them six officers and the two majors. The remainder were pursued into the forest, where most of them perished.

For his part, General Lévis, second-in-command in Canada, consigned the following account of Grant's defeat

Before leaving Carillon [Ticonderoga], we learned during the last days of October from [Governor] General Vaudreuil that an enemy detachment of 900 men commanded by Mr. Grant, major of one of the Scots battalions, and a major of [American] militia, had advanced up to canon range of Fort Duquesne to attack by surprise during the night the camp of the Canadians and the Indians we had at that place. The enemy detachment was at dawn sighted by our Indians who shouted and gave the alarm to the Canadians. Mr. De Lignery who was in command at that place ordered everyone under arms, which consisted of about 1,500 men, who marched at once towards the enemy [troops] who were very surprised to [see] such a large number. They thought we had no Indians and we had five to six hundred surrounding the enemy detachment, which was defeated in a short time. They had 500 men killed or captured; no more than 300 escaped the same fate by fleeing. Mr. Grant and the militia major were made prisoners with three [other] officers. We lost only 20 men killed or wounded." However, he went on to state that the prisoners said that General Forbes was advancing "with an army of 6,000 men to attack Fort Duquesne; that the detachment led by Mr. Grant was merely an advance guard sent to reconnoiter the road; that the army of General Forbes had taken a different road than that of [General] Braddock...and was entrenched at Royal-Hanon, about 18 leagues from Fort Duquesne.

These accounts, some of which appear to have been related verbally by men coming from the Ohio to officers in Canada, have many discrepancies on casualties and on who actually led the French force that attacked Grant's troops. With regard to leadership, Lignery was certainly the one who ordered the garrison mustered and led it out of the fort. One notes that this was done quite fast, within six minutes according to Du Verny, which indicates that all followed a plan that had been previously worked out to cope with such an alarm. Lignery most likely did not personally take part in the French attack, probably because he was more elderly and would remain in charge of the men left in the fort and its immediate area, notably the 200 men mentioned by Du Verny. Captain Aubry was the obvious choice to lead the column's charge as reported by J.C.B. and alluded to by Governor-General Vaudreuil. All the accounts are quite vague as to where the fighting occurred, other than being in the large area of the wooded hills east of the fort. J.C.B. is the only one that mentions the direction taken by the column led by Aubry and it makes perfect sense. In a true counter-guerrilla tactic, he outflanked and surprised his enemy. The rest of the French soldiers and Canadian militiamen at and near the fort were keeping the Anglo-Americans occupied along the edge of the woods while Aubry made his flank movement; they then also charged in when the Anglo-Americans were being attacked on their flank and rear. Indians were not initially involved in great numbers, but that must have changed as more and more crossed the river to join in the fight, their war cries and fearsome appearance surely adding to the terror that eventually overtook Grant's men. Grant tried to make a last stand and rally his men, but to no avail. The panic must have been considerable when one considers that many men – in an age when few knew how to swim – drowned trying to cross the river.

The French and Canadian casualties were obviously light, but certainly not as few as in J.C.B.'s account. Between 15 and 20 dead and wounded is probably in the right range. The Indian casualties are not reported, but they must have been light also. The Anglo-American casualties were very high. Out of 38 officers, 14 were killed, including Chief Engineer Rhor, 16 were wounded and escaped, and eight were taken prisoner, including majors Grant and Lewis. Of the 860 NCOs and enlisted men, there were some 335 killed, of which 187 were of the 77th Highlanders, 35 of the 60th, 62 of the 1st Virginia Regiment, 27 of the Maryland Provincials, 18 of the 2nd Pennsylvania, four from North Carolina Provincials, and two from the Lower Counties. Some 40 wounded other ranks managed to escape to safety with another 485 that were not wounded. The raiding force had suffered a forty percent loss, a bad "butcher's bill".

"My heart is broke," wrote General Forbes when he heard of this extraordinary French and Indian success over the Anglo-American army. But nothing further was done, and it seems everyone on the Anglo-American side tried to forget about this grand fiasco and probably suppress or make light of it. Eventually, Grant was released on October 14, 1758, and yet was never court-martialed for his truly bumbling and utterly confused leadership. It seems a pity because valuable tactical lessons would have been learned. However, General Forbes was a fellow Scot and historian Douglas R. Cubbison suspects a Scottish cover-up, a theory that the author of this book certainly entertains.

**OCTOBER 12
1758**

**Aubry's Raid on
Fort Ligonier**

AUBRY'S RAID ON FORT LIGONIER

In spite of the outstanding success in repulsing Grant's raiding force, there now could be no doubt in the minds of Lignery, his officers, and his men, that the powerful Anglo-American army was nevertheless irrevocably advancing towards Fort Duquesne thanks to its road-building and the methodical progress it could afford to take. With what must have seemed to the French like a nearly limitless amount of men, supplies and money, the Anglo-American army could afford to build strong positions along the way, the latest being Fort Ligonier. It was clear that Fort Duquesne would have to be abandoned sooner or later. Although allied Indians had greatly profited from Grant's fiasco, they now had increasing misgivings about the capacity of the "Great White Father" to prevail in this conflict and many

were leaving to go back to their homelands. Nevertheless, the French officers were not discouraged.

The latest action had shown again that, except for rangers, British and American troops were not apt to fight in forest warfare. On the contrary, the French commanders now mooted a raid on the new British Fort Ligonier at Loyalhanna, probably at the behest of Captain Aubry who would lead the raiding force. The French and Canadians certainly did not perceive that this would stop the Anglo-American army, but it might delay it and give them more time to evacuate by putting the enemy on the defensive. Allied Indians would also see there were still plenty of opportunities to fight and take booty for a few more weeks. Accordingly, a party of about 450 soldiers and Canadian militiamen with some 150 allied Indians marched out of Fort Duquesne under the command of Captain Aubry. By early morning on October 12, from the nearby hills, they could see Fort Ligonier surrounded by small tent cities punctuated by corrals for horses and bullocks. Aubry's attack plan is not recorded, as with much else on the French side of the 1758 Ohio campaign, but, from what is known of the action, it was the classic "hit unexpectedly, strike hard and fast, then cover," all of which was well led. With about 600 men, the attack could come from several directions and it obviously did, judging from the Anglo-American accounts.

At the time of the attack, Colonel Bouquet was away from Fort Ligonier and the senior officer present was Colonel Burd of the 2nd Pennsylvania. He appears to have believed that this was a small raid on the horse and bullock corrals and sent the small Maryland Battalion to scatter the raiders. The decision spelled disaster for that battalion, which suffered high casualties. It was a full-scale attack coming seemingly from several sides; even if it did not, the important thing in the Canadian raid tactic was that the enemy would believe it did. Aubry and his men achieved their objective; the Anglo-American soldiers ran for the fort. There probably were pockets of resistance, but the results of an outstandingly successful raid were there: a much larger force of British regular and American provincial soldiers was reduced to run for shelter from a smaller group of French colonial regulars, Canadian militiamen, and Indian warriors who now had all the leisure to ravage the abandoned camp around the fort. Although a map by American Colonel Burd mentions "the French army's line of attack" being to the east, where it quickly overcame the encampment of the Maryland and Carolina provincial troops, the main thrust seems to have been made on the lowlands at the southwest side of the fort, initially across Loyalhanna Creek. The accounts are somewhat imprecise on both sides. For instance, it has been said that the French raiding force neglected to seal the eastern side of the fort. Yet it overran the encampment of the Maryland and Carolina provincials detachments on that side. However, the fact that the east side of Fort Ligonier might not have been sealed, does not mean that the road leading into it was not a danger zone. General Lévis' journal adds an important sidelight to the operation with regards to the allied Indian warriors. Many of them, as was their habit, were waiting concealed to attack whatever traveled on that road and they struck gold that day by intercepting an incoming convoy.

FOLLOWING PAGES:
Aubry's raid on Fort Ligonier
The failure of Grant's raid had shown that the Anglo-American troops were unprepared for war on the frontier, unlike the woodcraft-wise French colonial troops, Canadian militiamen, and allied Indians. Captain Aubry pressed this advantage by mounting a raid on Fort Ligonier, the closest fort built by General Forbes' army. By early October, the fort was largely complete and surrounded by "tent cities" and fenced enclosures for horses and cattle. French, Canadian, and Indian raiding parties surrounded the fort and, with the garrison distracted by a clash between one of the parties and an Anglo-American patrol to the southwest, burst from cover, overrunning the camps. Faced by this sudden attack from small parties of French soldiers, Canadian militiamen and Indian warriors that were far more adept at hand-to-hand fighting, the Anglo-American troops fled back to the safety of the fort. It was an outstandingly successful raid.

Captain Pouchot's journal records news of the raid that was received in Fort Niagara. After the initial clash with the party of American provincial troops, Aubry's men pursued "those who had been put to flight, the French came across the small camp, took it by surprise and sent the garrison fleeing for the main retrenchment, which they only just reached in time." According to a marginal note in his journal, a French soldier entered a tent in the "small camp" during the attack "and found there an officer drinking his tea. He said to him: 'What's this then? Your comrades are fighting and you are sitting here in comfort. You don't deserve to live.' With one blow of an axe, he killed him. For two days [actually one day], M. Aubry formed a kind of blockade around it. He had 200 cattle or horses killed. Almost all our men returned [to Fort Duquesne] on horseback," related Pouchot.

General Montcalm wrote to his superior, Marshal Belle-Isle, that "Captain Aubry, of the Louisiana troops, has gained a tolerably considerable advantage there on the 12th [of October]. The enemy lost on the occasion a hundred and fifty men, killed, wounded and missing; they were pursued as far as a new fort called Royal Hannon [Ligonier], which they built at the head of the River d'Attique [Loyalhanna Creek]. We had only two men killed and seven wounded" (DCHNY, X: pp. 900-901). As noted above, General Lévis also had news of Aubry's raid. His journal mentioned that "a party of 600 men under the orders of M. Aubry, captain of the marine troops of Louisiana, [left Fort Duquesne] to disrupt the enemy during their [construction] work and to take some of its [supply] convoys. Mr. Aubry advanced with his detachment up to a half-league from Royal-Hanon [Fort Ligonier], where he came upon [an outer] guard of 50 men that retreated and he followed it up to entrenchments where the army of General Forbes

Fort Ligonier, 1762. This rare view of the fort was made by Lt. Archibald Blane of the 60th (Royal Americans) Regiment on June 30, 1762. It shows the east wall's gate and its horizontally laid logs, the location of the flagpole, and the tops of the buildings within. The pointed logs at the top of the walls in place in 1758 were apparently removed by the time this rendering was made. (Collection and photo: Fort Ligonier Museum, Ligonier, Pennsylvania)

John Ligonier, First Earl Ligonier, 1760. Lord Ligonier was commander-in-chief of the British army from 1757 to 1759, thus at the time of Forbes' advance in 1758, and Fort Ligonier was named in his honor. He became Master-General of the Ordnance from 1759 to 1762. (Portrait by Sir Joshua Reynolds. Collection and photo: Fort Ligonier Museum, Ligonier, Pennsylvania)

took up its arms, but without daring to come out [of the fort]. Mr. Aubry [and his men] shot at the entrenchment [with muskets] for the rest of the day and had everything outside burned; his Indians fell upon a convoy and took 300 heads of cattle or horses. It was estimated that the enemy lost over 200 men and we had only eight killed or wounded."

Aubry had never intended on a siege but on a raid, which is a very different operation. Normally, now having successfully surprised and driven the enemy inside its fort and destroyed its camp, it was time to leave before they would make a sortie or, even worse, a relief enemy force arrived on the scene. Instead, probably based on intelligence reports telling him that the troops in the fort seemed shocked and that no other enemy troops were seen approaching from the east, Aubry opted for a short blockade of the fort.

AUBRY'S RAID ON FORT LIGONIER

OCTOBER 12, 1758

With the Anglo-American forces on the back foot, Captain Aubry led a raiding party of 450 French soldiers and Canadian militiamen, supported by some 150 allied Indians, to within sight of Fort Ligonier. He divided his force into smaller groups and spread them out around the fort. As the raiding parties closed in, one across Loyalhanna Creek ran into an Anglo-American patrol of about 50 men and quickly put them to flight. With the element of suprise vanishing, French and Canadian forces erupted from all sides and attacked Fort Ligonier's outer camps. The Anglo-American troops were caught off-guard, outfought in hand-to-hand combat, and forced to flee to the safety of the fort's stockade. To the east, allied Indians fell upon a British convoy. Instead of swiftly withdrawing, as was usual after a successful raid, Aubry's force blockaded the fort, keeping twice their number bottled up. Some ineffective artillery fire was the garrison's only response – in the words of General Forbes, "above 1,500 effective men within… neither made one sortie or followed them half a yard". Hoping that an ambush could be sprung on any such sortie, the raiders lay in wait overnight, before riding back to Fort Duquesne with many captured horses.

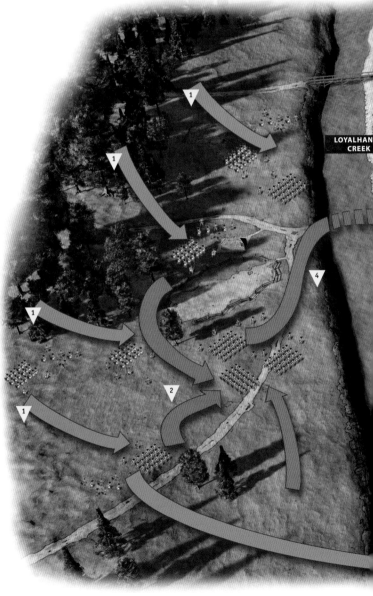

LOYALHAN
CREEK

EVENTS

1 Mixed groups of French soldiers and Canadian militiamen close around Fort Ligonier. To the east, allied Indians fan out to block the road.

2 One of the raiding groups skirmishes with an Anglo-American patrol.

3 The raiders launch their attack against the fort's outer camps.

4 British and American troops in the outer camps are surprised and outfought by the raiders, then forced back to the security of Fort Ligonier's stockades.

5 A British convoy is intercepted by the raiders.

6 Fort Ligonier becomes the refuge of some 1,500 British regular and American provincial soldiers.

FORT LIGONIER

He had limited numbers of French soldiers and Canadian militiamen to devote to such a static role. Every one of them was needed to face the numerous British and American troops, who simply remained safely huddled behind their field fortifications, not daring to come out.

That such a superior Anglo-American force should be reduced to a defensive position for over a day by a raiding party consisting of a few dozen regulars with a few hundred Canadian militiamen and Indians speaks for itself. General Forbes, who was in Fort Bedford at the time, recognized this in his report of the action to his superior, General Abercromby, stating that "above 1500 effective men within our breast work, exclusive of sick…neither made one Sortie or followed them half a yard, but shamefully" instead allowed the French and Indians to control everything outside Fort Ligonier. And, he added, "nor did we pursue one inch" after the enemy departed (this part of the dispatch was later stricken out as per WO 34/34). A pursuit might have been impractical although the Anglo-Americans probably were not fully aware of the main logistical reason. Lévis further wrote that "Mr. Aubry withdrew at dawn and, two days later, was back in Fort Duquesne." Aubry's force effectively blockaded Fort Ligonier for a night; the silence broken by Indian war whoops and the cannon fire and "a number of shells from our mortars" to keep the French and Indians at a safe distance, according to the October 26 issue of the *Pennsylvania Gazette* – a somewhat ironic comment considering the superior numbers of the Anglo-American garrison. Besides cattle, General Forbes mentioned the final inglorious event in that "all our horses" kept in corrals around Fort Ligonier were taken by the French. This allowed nearly all of them to ride back to a triumphal arrival at Fort Duquesne.

Lt. Corbière's patrol on November 12

This was not the last action that Fort Ligonier's garrison would experience. In early November Lt. Corbière, heading a party of about 40 to 45 soldiers, Canadian militiamen, and Indians, according to Pouchot, was lurking about in the forest near Fort Ligonier. Exact numbers and composition of his force are unknown, but a large one is unlikely; this was not a raiding party but a patrol to keep an eye on major Anglo-American movements at a time when Fort Duquesne's garrison was then being reduced. Indians that were formerly allied were much fewer and becoming neutral by the day. This was due to persistent efforts to convince the Indian nations in the Ohio to stop fighting with the French. General Forbes did not waste the authority over Indian diplomacy that Abercromby had bestowed upon him in July. Colonial officials were also anxious to arrive at an armistice with the native warriors, many of whom were now thinking that the French were just too weak to resist Anglo-American might in Pennsylvania. At another meeting at Easton in late October that was attended by many nations, the Delaware and other Ohio nations agreed to cease hostilities; an outcome due in no small measure to a letter by General Forbes addressed to the chiefs that called on them to return to their families and let the French and the English fight their own battles. This call for neutrality was undoubtedly greeted with relief and by early November Indian runners were dispatched to spread the word. This peace treaty was a tremendous advantage for Forbes' army, which would seal the fate of the French presence in the Ohio. Without the Indian allies, they were next to powerless.

But the French and Canadians could still be lethal. On November 12 Corbière and his men encountered a party – its strength is unknown – of American rangers patrolling at about three miles (5 km) from Fort Ligonier. He and his men probably did not know how strong the enemy party was, but in Canadian forest warfare numbers did not matter as much as gaining the element of surprise. Without hesitation, Corbière attacked the rangers, who ran back to the fort. General Forbes, who thought this was a raid on his army's horses and cattle, immediately sent 500 men to give chase to Corbière's party under colonels Mercer and Washington. Some of Mercer's men made contact with some of Corbière's men, shooting erupted in the forest near the fort, and, in the confusion and musket smoke, nervous Virginia Regiment soldiers started shooting at other indistinct shadows. They turned out to be their own men, and soon two groups of American troops were shooting at each other in a tragic case of friendly-fire. George Washington later recalled being never "in more imminent danger" in trying to stop the firing "between two [lines of] fire, knocking up with his sword" the pointed muskets. At least 11 men were killed and probably many more wounded on the Anglo-American side (Cubbison: p. 153). This time, however, some American provincials managed to capture three of Corbière's party including one Richard Johnson. What Forbes learned from him would change the entire operation against Fort Duquesne.

ANALYSIS

All three actions were remarkable for one common feature: when it came down to a tactical contest in the fast-moving action of forest warfare, the Anglo-American forces were consistently outfought. In this we are provided with an almost inconceivable textbook example of a campaign fought between numerous troops, whose quality there is no reason to doubt, but who were basically unsuited for wilderness operations in North America, and the small but highly specialized French, Canadian and Indian forces. To date, no written manual of the Canadian tactical doctrine has been found, but there can be little doubt that it was an outstanding combination of Indian skulking warfare tactics mixed with European organization and discipline. American rangers tried to emulate this during the Seven Years' War in North America, as witnessed by Major Rogers' famous ranging rules (published in 1765). The Canadians, however, had been mooting this type of warfare since the 1690s and, as seen above, trained their officer cadets to master all aspects by years spent participating in wilderness raids and residing among Indian nations.

On the other hand, General Forbes showed what could be done with a superior force more suited for an 18th-century European linear battle than any engagement in the wilderness, which, every time it occurred, ended up being an Anglo-American fiasco. But Forbes, unlike Braddock and Abercromby, did not venture to waste his advantage in the type of overconfident movement that brought defeat to both of those generals. For instance, Grant's disastrous raid would have never occurred had Forbes been at Fort Ligonier instead of Bouquet. General Forbes and his men were extremely lucky that the forces they had to face were so very much smaller than their own. Even as he lamented repeatedly on the shortcomings of his army when engaged against a far weaker enemy, he trusted in the power of his superior numbers and, most of all, of his limitless logistics to achieve his objective. In the case of securing the Ohio, his recipe was the correct one.

CONCLUSION

Richard Johnson was possibly a deserter who had joined the French or even a captive adopted by the Indians. He was now very eager to be helpful to General Forbes. On the evening of November 12, he gave a very detailed account of the pitiful state of Fort Duquesne, that its garrison was reduced to about 200 men and that supplies were running short. Upon hearing this, Forbes, who had previously opted to cease operations of his army as far as Fort Ligonier, immediately changed his mind and now issued orders to advance towards Fort Duquesne.

On the morning of November 23, the Anglo-American army was very near Fort Duquesne. In his report to Versailles, Governor-General Vaudreuil summed up the situation at Fort Duquesne since mid-November. Many men had been evacuated elsewhere and the garrison was now less than 300 men, "a third of whom at the most were capable of taking the field." There was obviously no point in trying to resist against such a strong force. Lignery and his officers all agreed that evacuation was the only option left. On November 19 some of the pickets around the fort were dismantled while Lignery had a formal inventory made of the remaining supplies in the fort; eighteen days' rations were sent to Illinois and nine days' rations went to the feeble Fort Machault, which was "so badly sited that one could see everything that went on [in] it from the top of the nearby mountains." He had previously shipped Fort Duquesne's artillery and ammunition to Illinois along with the sick and wounded men. Some 17,500 pounds of corn and 5,840 pounds of tobacco were left in the fort. On November 23, as the British approached, the remaining 192 officers and men left the fort and boarded bateaux. "When everyone had embarked, when the scouts had returned, and when all the bateaux had left, except one which he [Lignery] had kept, he had the fort set on fire… To blow up the fort, 50 or 60 barrels of spoilt powder were left in the powder magazine. As soon as M. de Lignery heard the explosion of this mine, he sent three men by land to see what damage it had done. They reported that the fort was entirely reduced to ashes and that the enemy would find

NOVEMBER 23 1758

Fort Duquesne blown up by French garrison

MARCH 11 1759

Death of Gen. Forbes

nothing but the ironwork of its buildings" (Colonies, C11A, 104: p.13). Sure enough, what remained of Fort Duquesne were its charred ruins when Forbes and his troops at last reached the fork of the Ohio River.

News of the loss of Fort Duquesne reached Montreal about six weeks later. According to Malartic's journal, "two officers arrived from Fort Duquesne" on January 10, 1759 at ten o'clock at night with this news. For Governor-General Vaudreuil and General Montcalm, a substantial part of the southwestern area south of Lake Erie had fallen. Sooner or later, forts Machault, Le Boeuf, and de la Presqu'île would have to be evacuated and destroyed if Forbes' army came up the Alleghany River in the spring or summer. That would hamper communications with Detroit, Michilimackinac, Louisiana, and the western Great Lakes, but it would not cut them off because the main route to those places was by the Ottawa and Madawaska rivers to the northern shores of Lake Huron. More worrying was that the Anglo-American army that had failed to take Ticonderoga would surely try again in 1759 and, in the worst-case scenario, the army and fleet that had taken Louisbourg would next appear before Quebec. The meager French forces in Canada were only able to face the attack on one front. Certainly Vaudreuil and Montcalm must have felt increasingly hemmed in when they heard that Fort Duquesne had fallen.

Following the arrival of the Anglo-American army on the site of the charred remains of Fort Duquesne, parties of troops started to fan out to secure its immediate area. There were many abandoned Indian encampments in the vicinity and American provincial troops are said to have come to an Indian race path, which was also used to subject their hapless prisoners to run the gauntlet. This particular path, however, was truly macabre because on each side of it were stakes with the bark peeled off, each one with the head and the kilt of a Highlander upon it. Following the provincials was a party of the 77th, whose men flew into a rage at this sight. "Directly, a rapid and violent trampling was heard, and immediately the whole corps of Highlanders, with their muskets abandoned and broadswords drawn, rushed by the Provincials, foaming with rage, swearing vengeance and extermination upon the French troops who had permitted such outrages. But the French had fled…" (quoted in Albert's *Frontier Forts*).

This incident, typical of warfare involving Indians in North America, shows the frustration of the men of 77th, for in previous engagements with the "French and Indians" they had been made to run for their lives. Some of those who did not make it had a quick end or suffered unspeakable tortures before giving up the soul. This was the terrifying prospect when campaigning in the wilderness. The French settlers and soldiers in Canada were subject to this sort of threat too since the early 17th century from their Indian enemies, especially the Iroquois, and even from some allied warriors that were disappointed or drinking heavily. But many Indian nations were also allies and the French knew they could not rule the wilderness without their assistance. The Indian's ceremonial practices towards prisoners they chose for these purposes were as barbaric to French eyes as they were to any other Europeans'. However, the British and Americans did not need the Indians as much as the French did; this was especially true during the Seven Years' War when many troops came from Europe and many provincial units were raised in the colonies. From the late 17th century French officers would try to buy off English or American prisoners, and had special funds allotted to do this. Nevertheless, the Indians often elected to keep their prisoners, who either suffered agony or were adopted. Those redeemed by the French were the "New England captives," some of whom left harrowing tales of their ordeals. For their part, French soldiers and Canadian settlers knew they were as good as dead if they were so unlucky as to be captured by enemy Indians. The bonuses offered in the American colonies for live prisoners were almost the same as the price of scalps, so captured individuals were killed; thus, unless they were adopted, no New France captives survived to tell their tales.

At the site of Fort Duquesne now occupied by the Anglo-American army, it was late November and the winter would soon arrive. On November 25, all troops were to attend a divine service to give thanks to God for the army's success. Thereafter, the troops looked for and found in the vicinity many skeletons and remains of men that had fallen over three years before with Braddock, and more recently with Grant, to give them a proper burial. The site of the destroyed Fort Duquesne would of course remain occupied by a regular garrison. Although the French had gone, they

Evacuation of Fort Duquesne, November 1758. (Print after W. Snyder. Private collection. Author's photo)

A sickly but content and happy General Forbes gazes at the destroyed Fort Duquesne while writing his report that the place has at last been occupied by the Anglo-American army. In the distance the heads of the Monongahela and Alleghany rivers are forming the Ohio River. The high hill at left is the present Mount Washington. The uniform worn by Forbes is somewhat erroneous: the shoulder epaulettes were not introduced in the British forces until ten years later. (Painting by Nat Youngblood. Fort Pitt Museum, Pittsburg. Author's photo)

might be so bold as to come back and reoccupy the site if the Anglo-Americans ever left – an unthinkable prospect. Therefore, a new fort had to be immediately built on the spot to protect its garrison from the elements of winter's cold and snows. The army started construction to erect a small new bastioned stockade post that was only 145 feet to each side and located about a thousand feet further back from the former French fort. Some material from the charred French fort was recuperated, and by adding its own building supplies and new logs the new fort was on the way to completion by mid-December.

Most British and American troops started heading east while smaller garrisons remained in the forts along what had become known as Forbes Road. For his part, Brigadier-General Forbes was desperately ill and departed on December 4 for the long trip back to Philadelphia, where his failing health would be attended to. Many troops were also heading back, but a few hundred would remain. Before leaving, according to the London *Universal Chronicle* of April 7–14, 1759, General Forbes "appointed Capt. Alexander McKenzie of Dalmour, of Col. Montgomery's Highland regiment, to be the Governor of the fort and that he had under his command 200 of Montgomery's Highland battalion, and 300 picked Provincials, all in good health and high spirits, and under no apprehension

of danger" and that "General Forbes was to return from Philadelphia the beginning of April, to rebuild the fort." The fort was indeed rebuilt to a much larger size, but General Forbes did not return. His ailment continued to worsen. On the morning of Sunday, March 11, 1759, he passed away in Philadelphia, which, as Bouquet remarked, at last "put an end to his miseries" and sufferings, at age 51. He was appreciated and respected not only by military men, but also by many Pennsylvanians. Therefore, his funeral in Philadelphia three days later was a major ceremony in the city, and his body was laid to rest in Christ Church where it remains today.

The other main actors of the campaign either disappeared from the pages of history or went on to great glory. The latter was the fate of Colonel Washington, who was destined to be revered as the father of the United States of America and its first president. Lignery did not disappear immediately from the Ohio area, but remained for the winter of 1758–59 with a small force of regulars and militiamen at Fort Machault. From there, he sponsored small Indian raids to keep the Anglo-Americans on their guard, and by the late spring of 1759 was planning a major raid on the larger Fort Pitt, which the British were starting to build at Pittsburgh. However, the commander of Fort Niagara was being besieged by another Anglo-American army and appealed for help. Lignery came with a relief

Destruction of Fort de la Presqu'île, 1759. Following their evacuation and destruction of Fort Duquesne, forts Machault (or Venango), Le Boeuf, and de la Presqu'île were also set on fire by the retreating French and Canadians. (Anonymous 1930s painting. Erie County Historical Society, Erie, Pennsylvania. Author's photo)

column, but was ambushed and defeated by an Anglo-Indian force on July 24. The fort capitulated the next day and Lignery, who had been wounded and made prisoner, died of his wounds three days later. Captain Aubry was also made prisoner and exchanged in 1760. In 1763 he was back in Louisiana as commandant of the small French garrison that waited for years for the Spanish to take over the colony, which had been ceded to them by France in compensation for their loss of Florida to the British. Aubry became acting governor and managed some tense political issues until the Spanish finally arrived in force at New Orleans during 1769. With some French residents and soldiers who wished to go back to France, he boarded the ship *Père de famille* but it was caught in a storm as it neared Bordeaux and, on February 4, 1770, foundered on the rocky French coast. All on board were lost, save the ship's captain, a physician, a sergeant of the Louisiana troops, and two sailors who succeeded in reaching land safely. The premature deaths of Lignery and, especially, Aubry probably meant the loss of document and of memoirs that would never be written about the events of 1758 in particular.

FURTHER READING AND SELECT BIBLIOGRAPHY

The 1758 campaign did not result in a huge number of historical studies. Even primary source accounts are not abundant and the published documents mainly concern General Forbes', Colonel Bouquet's, and Colonel Washington's correspondence and orders. This is largely because of more spectacular campaigns going on elsewhere, which have attracted more inspiration by historians. Still, Americans have contributed fine studies on various aspects ranging from military accounts to the research and reconstructions of forts and other features built along Forbes Road. The British in the United Kingdom have had some slight interest, but were and remain more concerned by other campaigns throughout their empire. As for the French in France, they understandably have not been inspired by a minor campaign in a lost war that, to this day, does not raise much interest in metropolitan France. Canadian studies have somewhat followed the same trends, those in anglophone Canada feeling victoriously smug and centering on General Wolfe and 1759, while those in francophone Canada see the War of the Conquest (*la guerre de la conquête* – French Canada's name for the Seven Years' War in North America) as a sort of historic nightmare that brought defeat in spite of a stubborn defense, abandonment by the mother country, and permanent cession to an enemy power. Another reason for the paucity of participants' accounts and studies is that Forbes, Grant, Lignery, and Aubry all died during or shortly after the war, leaving no detailed memoirs. Thus only a small number of participants' papers remain.

Primary source official documents can be found in The National Archives (formerly the Public Records Office) at Kew, United Kingdom, especially in the War Office (referred to as WO) 34 series, and the Colonial Office (CO) 5 series. France's Archives Nationales center for overseas documents is at Aix-en-Provence in the Colonies section, mostly in the B, C11A, and C11B series, although some pertinent documents can also be found in other centers, sections, and series.

Published works

Albert, George Dallas, *The Frontier Forts of Pennsylvania*, State Printer, Harrisburg (1916), 2 vols

Anderson, Fred, *The Crucible of War*, Vintage Books, New York (2000). Remarkable for its account of Indian diplomacy.

Bouquet, Henry, *The Papers of Henry Bouquet*, edited by S.K. Stevens, Donald H. Kent, and Autumn L. Leonard. Pennsylvania Historical and Museum Commission, Harrisburg, Volume I (1972) and Volume II (1951)

Cubbison, Douglas R, *The British Defeat of the French in Pennsylvania 1758*, McFarland, Jefferson, NC (2010). An excellent account of the campaign against Fort Duquesne as seen from the British and colonial American sources, points of view, and analysis. It quotes many essential documents including those from the unpublished papers of Forbes' headquarters at the University of Virginia. However, this study does not offer much in the way of the French and Canadian sides' points of view and analysis because very few French and Canadian sources seem to have been consulted, even when they were translated into English. It is nevertheless an extremely useful, essential, and much recommended study.

Documents Relative to the Colonial History of the State of New York, edited by E.B. O'Callaghan, Albany (1858), Volume X. In spite of its title, it contains many documents by New France officers that mention Fort Duquesne and Pennsylvania translated into English.

Forbes, John, *Letters of General John Forbes relating to the expedition against Fort Duquesne in 1758*, compiled by Irene Stewart, Pittsburgh (1927)

Forbes, John, *Writings of General John Forbes*, edited by Alfred Proctor James, Collegiate Press, Menasha, Wisconsin (1938)

Fournier, Marcel, ed. *Combattre pour la France en Amérique: Les soldats de la guerre de Sept Ans en Nouvelle-France 1755–1760*, Société généalogique canadienne-française, Montréal (2009). Exhaustive statistics and nominal lists of French troops in Canada.

J.C.B., *Voyage au Canada fait depuis l'an 1751 jusqu'en l'an 1761*, Aubier Montaigne, Paris (1978). In this account the author describes himself as a gunner nicknamed "Jolicoeur" in the regular colonial artillery company (the "Canonniers-Bombardiers") in Canada. His initials and nickname are the only ones that correspond to one of the gunners sent to the Ohio in 1754. He was thus Joseph Charles Bonin. He was literate so he was a Fort Duquesne storekeeper by 1758. His account was first published in Quebec City by Father Casgrain in 1887, who cut some of the original text and erroneously identified him as Lieutenant J.-C. de Bonnefois of the metropolitan Royal-Artillerie. The 1978 edition was made from the original manuscript in the Paris Bibliothèque Nationale. Although J.C.B. did not take part in fighting Grant's raid, he was in Fort Duquesne when the raid occurred and later transcribed what he recalled hearing of it. His account appears to have been consigned mainly in the

1790s. He does mix up dates and some events, but his account is validated and outstanding on daily life, with certain details that could only have been known by being a witness.

Lévis, Gaston de, *Journal des campagnes du chevalier de Lévis en Canada de 1756 à 1760*, edited by H.-R. Casgrain, Quebec (1889)

Malartic, Anne-Joseph Maures de Malartic, *Journal de campagne au Canada*, Dijon (1890)

McConnell, David, *British Smoothbore Artillery: a Technological Survey*, Canadian Parks Service, Ottawa (1988). Exhaustive and outstanding study.

Montcalm, Louis-Joseph, *Journal du Marquis de Montcalm durant ses campagnes au Canada de 1756 à 1759*, edited by H.-R. Casgrain, Quebec (1895)

Papiers Contrecoeur, edited by Fernand Grenier, Université Laval, Québec (1952)

Pouchot, Pierre, *Memoirs of the Late War in North America Between France and Britain*, translated by Michael Cary, annotated and edited by Brian L. Dunnigan, Old Fort Niagara Association, Youngstown, NY (1994)

Stotz, Charles Morse, *Outposts of the War for Empire*, Historical Society of Pennsylvania and University of Pittsburgh Press (1985). Outstanding and classic study.

INDEX

References to illustrations are shown in **bold**.

Abercromby, LtGen Sir James 21, **22**, 25, 35, 46, 68, 70
Albert, George Dallas 72
Amherst, MajGen Jeffery 21, 25, 35
Anglo-American forces 12–13, 14–15, 16–17, 20–23
  60th Regiment 15, 25, 26, 28, **28**, **29**, 59
  77th Regiment (Highlanders) 16, 26–27, **33**, 52, **58**, 59, 72, 74
  American provincial troops 28–32, 34, 59, 61, 72, 74
    Pennsylvania Regiment 32, 34, **36**, 38–39, 40, 59, 61
    Virginia Regiments 11, 29, 31, **36**, 39, 59, 69
  Board of Ordnance 27, 28
  British fleet 21
  Forbes' army 4, 18, 25–34
  militia 11, 14, 15, 16–17, **17**
  Royal Artillery 27
Armstrong, Col John 32, 34
Aubry, Capt Charles-Philippe 46, 47, 56, 57, 59, 76
  raid on Fort Ligonier 60–68, **62–63**, **66–67**

Belle-Isle, Marshal 64–65
Boscawen, Adm Edward 21
Bougainville, Louis-Antoine de 57
Bouquet, LtCol Henry 25, **25**, 26, 28, 61, 75
  advance on Fort Duquesne 37, 38–40, 42–43, 49
  Grant's raid 52, 53, 70
Braddock, Gen Edward 4, 14–15, 18, 19, 27, 70, 73
Braddock Road **24**, 35, 37, 39–40, 48, 52, 57
British American colonies 5, **5**, 12–14, 15, 16
  see also Anglo-American forces; Great Britain; Indian nations
Bullet, Captain 53
Burd, Col James 34, 36–37, 61
Byrd, Col William 31

Canada 5, 6, 7, 8, 16, 17, 72
  conquest of 18–19, **19**
Canadian officers 7, 8–9, 10, 15, 46, 70
Céloron de Blainville, Capt Pierre Joseph 10
Chew, Capt Colby 39, 42
Clayton, Capt Asher 39
Corbière, Lt 68–69
Coulon de Villiers, Capt Louis 12
Croghan, George 42–43, 47
Cubbison, Douglas R. 4, 39, 59, 69

Delaware nation 20, 35, 68
Dieskau, Baron 20
Dinwiddie, Robert 11, 31
Doreil, Commissary General 47, 48
Du Verny 56–57, 58–59
Duquesne, Governor-General 10, 11

European war 15–16

Forbes' campaign (1758)
  Aubry's raid 60–68, **62–63**, **66–67**
  Forbes' army 4, 18, 25–34
  Grant's raid 4, 49–59, **50–51**, 52, 53, **54–55**, 59, 70, 73
  Lt. Corbière's patrol 68–69
  routes to Fort Duquesne **24**, 35–40, 42
  strength of Fort Duquesne garrison 42–43, 46–48
  see also Indian nations; strategy
Forbes, Gen John 4, **23**, **24**, **32**, 74
  on artillery 27–28
  on Aubry's raid 68

biography 22–23, 26
  conflict with George Washington 40, 42
  on Fort Duquesne garrison 42–43
  on Grant's raid 52, 59, 70
  ill health and death 23, 52, 74–75
  on strategy with Indian nations 35, 68
  on warfare 37–38, 70
Forbes' Road 39, **42**, **43**, 74
Fort Bedford 36, **38**, 39, **40**, 49, 52, 68
Fort de la Presqu'ile 10–11, 72, 75
Fort Duquesne **49**
  evacuation and destruction 60, 68, 69, 71–72, **73–74**, **73**, **74**
  garrison 42–43, 46–48
  routes **24**, 35–40, 42
  strategic importance 11–12, 19, 20
  see also Braddock, Gen Edward; Grant, Maj James
Fort Ligonier 4, 52, **60**, **64**
  Aubry's raid 60–68, **62–63**, **66–67**
  Lt. Corbière's patrol 68–69
Fort Machault 11, 71, 72, 75
Fort Necessity 12, 14, 31
Fort Niagara 14, 57, 64, 75–76
Fort Ticonderoga (Carillon) 4, 21, 22, 35, 46, 72
France 5, **5**, 15–16
  see also French/New France forces; New France
Franklin, Benjamin 30, 32
French and Indian War (1754–1763) 4, 12
French/New France forces 6–8, 10–11, 14–15, 17, 21–22
  Canonniers-Bombardiers 10
  Compagnies Franches de la Marine 7, 8, 10, 14, **41**, **44**, **45**, 46, 57
  Fort Duquesne garrison 42–43, 46–48
  militia 7, 8, 10, 12, 17, 46
  militia (Canadian) 8, 10, 12, 14, 47, 57–59, 61, 68–69

George II, King of Great Britain and Ireland 15, 20
Grant, Maj James 4, 49–59, **50–51**, 52, 53, **54–55**, 59, 70, 73
Great Britain 5, **5**, 14–15, 20–21
  see also Anglo-American forces; British American colonies
Great Peace of Montreal (1701) 8

Halkett, Col Francis 25, 40
Hampshire County skirmishes **17**
Hay, CaptLt David 34

Indian nations
  relations with British colonies 18, 19–20, 31, 34–35, 68–69
  relations with French colonies 7–8, 10, 19-20, **21**, 60–61
Indian warriors **9**, 10, **12**, **17**, 72–73
Iroquois nation 10, 20, 35, 72
Isle Royale 5, 6, 7, 8
  see also Louisbourg

J.C.B. 46, 47, 57, 59
Johnson, Richard 69, 71
Johnson, Sir William 20, 35
Jumonville, Ensign Joseph Coulon de Villiers, Sieur de 12
Jumonville Glen, battle of (1754) 8, 11–12, 31

La Salle, Robert Cavelier de 10
Le Moyne d'Iberville, Pierre 10
League of Six Nations 19–20
Lévis, Gen Gaston de 58, 61, 64, 68
Lewis, Maj Andrew 52, 53, 57, 59
Lignery, François-Marie Marchand de 46, 47, 48, 53, 56, 58–59, 60, 71–72, 75–76

Ligonier, John **65**
Loudon, John Campbell, Earl of 18–19, **18**, 20, 21, 23
Louisbourg 14, 15, 17, 19, 21, 22
  see also Isle Royale
Louisbourg, battle of (1758) 4, 35
Louisiana 5, 6–7, 8, 11, 46, 72, 76

Macarty, Commandant 46, 47
Malartic, Anne-Joseph Maures de 72
Marin de la Malgue, Capt Paul 10
Maryland 11, 13, 15, 34, 35
McDonald, Captain 52
McKenzie of Dalmour, Capt Alexander 74
Mercer, Col Hugh 34, 69
Monceau 12
Monongahela, battle of (1755) 4, **16**, 18, 19, 20, 25, 29, 31, 46
Montcalm, Gen Louis-Joseph de 15, 35, 48, 56, 64–65, 72
Montgomery, Archibald 26
Montreal 7, 8, 10, 19, 20, 47

New France 5, **5**, 6–11, 15
  see also France; French/New France forces; Indian nations
New York 5, 13, 14, 19–20
North America, map (1750s) **5**

Ohio Valley (before Forbes campaign) 8, 10–12, **12**, 14–15
Oswego 15

Pemberton, Israel 35
Pennsylvania 11, 13, 15, 21
  see also Forbes campaign (1758); Quakers
Pennsylvania Gazette 52, 68
Pitt, William 15, 20–21, 22, 23, 38
Pouchot, Capt Pierre 57–58, 64, 68

Quakers 11, 13, 27, 32
Quebec City 6, 7, 8, 11, 14, 19, 72

raids see Forbes' campaign (1758)
Rhor, Chief Engineer Charles 28, 39, 59
road-building 4, 14, 28, 37, 38–39, 49
Rogers, Maj Robert 70

Saint-Pierre, Captain 11
Seven Years' War (1756–1763) 5, 8, 15, 30, 70, 73
Spain/New Spain 5, **5**, 75
St. Clair, LtCol Sir John 25, **26**, 31, 38, 39
Stewart of Garth 26
strategy 18–23
  see also Forbes' campaign (1758); Indian nations

Treaty of Easton (1758) 35, 68–69
Treaty of Utrecht (1713) 6
Troyes, Chevalier de 10

Universal Chronicle 74

Vaudreuil, Governor-General 53, 56, 59, 71, 72
Virginia 11, 13, 14, 15, **17**

Ward, Capt Edward 39
warfare (Anglo-American forces) 13, 37–38, 70
warfare (French/New France forces) 7, 8, 10, 15, 46–47, 70, 72–73
Washington, Col George **13**, **16**, 75
  conflict with Forbes 40, 42
  Jumonville Glen 11–12
  Lt. Corbière's patrol 69
  Virginia Provincials 29, 30, 31
weapons 7, 27–28, **30**, **31**, 34